GRAMMAR WORKBOOK

EXERCISES in ENGLISH

Teacher Guide

LEVEL

F

LOYOLAPRESS.

CHICAGO

The Workout That Brings Mastery in Grammar, Usage, and Mechanics

Exercises in English is the perfect teaching tool for educators who want their students to be educationally fit and READY—ready to communicate effectively when writing or speaking, ready for everyday language arts tasks, ready for accelerated English-language learning, and ready for assessment. Here are some ways that a workout with Exercises in English helps students become READY for any language arts task that they encounter:

RIGOROUS PRACTICE

Students are provided with a multitude of exercises on each page. With so many opportunities for learning, "practice makes perfect" is achievable!

EXAMPLES AND DEFINITIONS

Success comes with systematic instruction. Each new grammar, usage, or mechanics concept is clearly explained through examples and definitions.

ASSESSMENT

GUM scores increase as students are assessed and master their work with sentences, verbal agreement, and punctuation.

DIAGRAMMING FOR IN-DEPTH LANGUAGE STUDY

When students diagram sentences, they create visual representations of their learning—they can actually see how words work together to make correctly constructed sentences.

YEARLONG REINFORCEMENT FOR LEARNERS AT EVERY LEVEL

With six books of varying levels and a multitude of lessons in each book, students are provided with learning opportunities that last a full school year and beyond.

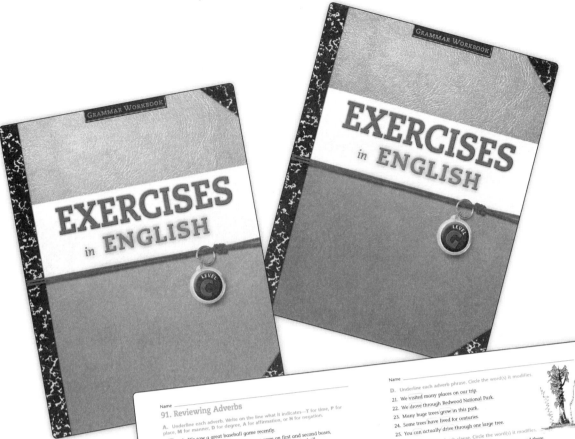

Inside Exercises in English

RIGOROUS PRACTICE

Focused skills are practiced in a variety of ways.

EXAMPLES AND DEFINITIONS

Clear definitions and numerous examples guide instruction.

Level of difficulty increases as students complete each section of a page.

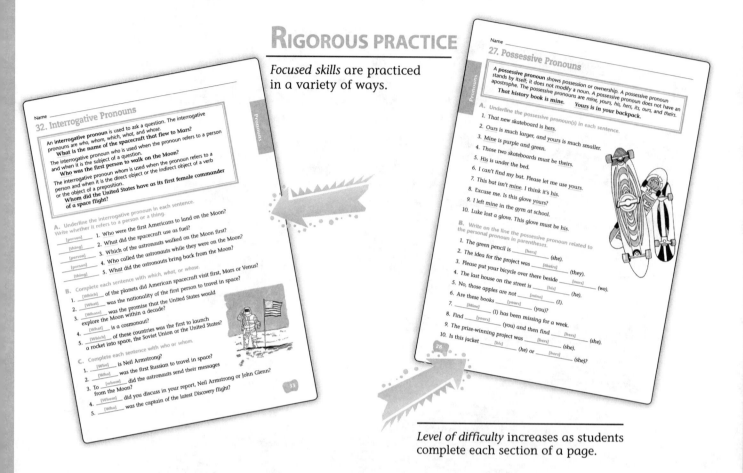

ASSESSMENT

Comprehensive reviews allow for classroom assessment or preparation for standardized tests.

DIAGRAMMING FOR IN-DEPTH LANGUAGE STUDY

Sentence diagramming helps students better understand and remember concepts.

YEARLONG REINFORCEMENT FOR LEARNERS AT EVERY LEVEL

Leveled books allow for differentiated instruction. Determine which books to use based on individual student achievement rather than grade level.

Handbook of Terms invites all learners to refresh and expand their knowledge.

Mastery and More

When teachers and students use *Exercises in English,* they receive more than any other language arts workout offers.

Teachers receive MORE with

- easy-to-grade exercises that are always in multiples of five.

- perforated pages for easy grading and portfolio storage.

- embedded answers that make correcting a breeze.

Students receive MORE with

- grammar, mechanics, and usage lessons that support *Voyages in English.*

- cross-curricular content for reinforcement and enrichment in social studies and science.

- character-education lessons with positive role models as examples.

- practice in context for authentic writing opportunities and self-assessment.

Comprehensive Scope and Sequence

Review the Scope and Sequence on pages T7–T11 to note how skill instruction is scaffolded across levels. Use the level or levels that best meet your students' needs.

Exercises in English—Scope and Sequence

SENTENCES	C	D	E	F	G	H
The Four Kinds of Sentences	✔	✔	✔	✔	✔	✔
Subjects and Predicates	✔	✔	✔	✔	✔	✔
Simple Subjects and Predicates		✔		✔	✔	✔
Compound Subjects and Predicates		✔	✔	✔	✔	✔
Direct Objects		✔	✔	✔	✔	✔
Complete Subjects and Predicates			✔	✔	✔	✔
Natural and Inverted Order in Sentences			✔	✔	✔	✔
Indirect Objects				✔	✔	✔
Compound Sentences				✔	✔	✔
Complex Sentences					✔	✔
Compound Complex Sentences						✔
NOUNS	C	D	E	F	G	H
Proper and Common Nouns	✔	✔	✔	✔	✔	
Singular and Plural Nouns	✔	✔	✔	✔	✔	✔
Possessive Nouns	✔	✔	✔	✔	✔	✔
Nouns Used as Subjects		✔	✔	✔		✔
Nouns Used as Objects		✔	✔	✔	✔	✔
Count and Noncount Nouns		✔	✔	✔		✔
Nouns Used as Subject Complements			✔	✔	✔	✔
Nouns Used in Direct Address			✔	✔		
Nouns Used as Objects of Prepositions			✔	✔	✔	✔
Appositives				✔	✔	✔
Collective Nouns				✔	✔	
Concrete and Abstract Nouns				✔	✔	
Words Used as Nouns and Verbs				✔		
Nouns Used as Object Complements						✔
VERBS	C	D	E	F	G	H
Regular and Irregular Verbs	✔	✔	✔	✔	✔	✔
Present Tense	✔	✔	✔	✔	✔	✔
Progressive Tenses	✔	✔	✔	✔	✔	✔
Past Tense	✔	✔	✔	✔	✔	✔
Future Tenses	✔	✔	✔	✔	✔	✔
Action Verbs	✔	✔	✔			
Verbs of Being	✔	✔	✔			
Helping Verbs	✔	✔				
Forms of *Bring*	✔					

	C	D	E	F	G	H
Forms of *Buy*	✔					
Forms of *Come*	✔					
Forms of *Eat*	✔					
Forms of *Go*	✔		✔			
Forms of *See*	✔		✔			
Forms of *Sit* and *Set*	✔		✔	✔		
Forms of *Take*	✔		✔			
Forms of *Write*	✔					
Forms of *To Be*	✔	✔	✔			
Forms of *Begin*		✔				
Forms of *Break*		✔	✔			
Forms of *Choose*		✔	✔			
Forms of *Do*		✔				
Verb Phrases		✔	✔	✔	✔	
Intransitive Verbs (Linking Verbs)		✔	✔	✔	✔	✔
There Is and *There Are*		✔		✔	✔	
Subject-Verb Agreement			✔	✔	✔	✔
Transitive Verbs			✔	✔	✔	✔
Doesn't and *Don't*			✔	✔	✔	✔
Let and *Leave*			✔	✔		
Teach and *Learn*			✔			
Lie and *Lay*			✔	✔		
Rise and *Raise*				✔		
Perfect Tenses				✔	✔	
Words Used as Nouns and Verbs					✔	
Active and Passive Voice					✔	✔
Modal Auxiliary Verbs					✔	✔
You Are and *You Were*					✔	
Compound Tenses						✔
Emphatic Verb Forms						✔
PRONOUNS	C	D	E	F	G	H
Singular and Plural Pronouns	✔	✔	✔			
Subject Pronouns	✔	✔	✔	✔	✔	✔
Possessive Pronouns	✔	✔	✔	✔	✔	✔
I and *Me*	✔	✔				
Pronouns Used as Subject Complements	✔		✔	✔	✔	✔
Pronouns Used as Direct Objects		✔	✔	✔	✔	✔
The Person of Pronouns		✔	✔	✔		
The Gender of Pronouns			✔			

We and *Us*		✔				
Pronouns Used as Objects of Prepositions			✔	✔		
Pronouns Used in Contractions			✔	✔		
Reflexive Pronouns			✔	✔	✔	
Interrogative Pronouns				✔	✔	✔
Indefinite Pronouns				✔	✔	✔
Double Negatives				✔		
Pronouns Used as Indirect Objects					✔	✔
Who and *Whom*					✔	✔
Pronouns Used After *Than* and *As*					✔	✔
Relative Pronouns					✔	✔
Demonstrative Pronouns					✔	✔
Nothing and *Anything*					✔	
Pronouns Used as Objects of Prepositions						✔
Intensive Pronouns			✔			✔

ADJECTIVES	C	D	E	F	G	H
Descriptive Adjectives	✔			✔	✔	✔
Adjectives That Tell How Many	✔	✔	✔	✔		
Indefinite and Definite Articles	✔	✔	✔	✔	✔	
Demonstrative Adjectives	✔	✔	✔	✔	✔	✔
Comparative Forms of Adjectives	✔	✔	✔	✔	✔	✔
Possessive Adjectives		✔	✔	✔		
Common and Proper Adjectives		✔	✔			✔
Good and *Bad*		✔				
The Position of Adjectives			✔	✔	✔	✔
Superlative Forms of Adjectives			✔	✔	✔	✔
Adjectives Used as Subject Complements				✔		
Words Used as Adjectives or Nouns				✔	✔	✔
Those and *Them*				✔		
Interrogative Adjectives				✔		✔
Few and *Little*					✔	✔

ADVERBS	C	D	E	F	G	H
Adverbs of Time	✔	✔	✔	✔		
Adverbs of Place	✔	✔	✔	✔		
Good and *Well*	✔	✔	✔			
Comparative Adverbs		✔	✔	✔		✔
Adverbs of Manner		✔	✔	✔		
No, Not, and *Never*		✔	✔	✔		
Superlative Adverbs			✔	✔		
Real and *Very*			✔			

	C	D	E	F	G	H
Their and *There*			✔	✔		
To, Too, and *Two*			✔	✔		
Adverbs and Adjectives				✔	✔	✔
There, Their, and *They're*					✔	
Farther and *Further*					✔	✔
Interrogative Adverbs					✔	✔
Adverbial Nouns					✔	✔
As . . . As, So . . . As, and *Equally*						✔

PUNCTUATION, CAPITALIZATION, ABBREVIATIONS	C	D	E	F	G	H
End Punctuation	✔	✔	✔	✔	✔	✔
Periods After Abbreviations, Titles, and Initials	✔	✔				
Capital Letters	✔	✔	✔	✔	✔	
Titles of Books and Poems	✔		✔	✔	✔	
Commas Used in Direct Address	✔	✔	✔	✔		
Punctuation in Direct Quotations	✔	✔	✔	✔		
Apostrophes		✔	✔			
Commas After *Yes* and *No*		✔	✔	✔		
Commas Separating Words in a Series		✔	✔	✔		
Commas After Parts of a Letter			✔	✔		
Commas in Dates and Addresses			✔	✔		
Commas in Geographical Names			✔			
Commas Used with Appositives				✔		
Commas Used in Compound Sentences				✔		
Semicolons and Colons				✔	✔	✔
Apostrophes, Hyphens, and Dashes				✔	✔	✔
Commas and Semicolons						✔

PREPOSITIONS, CONJUNCTIONS, INTERJECTIONS	C	D	E	F	G	H
Prepositions and Prepositional Phrases			✔	✔	✔	✔
Interjections			✔	✔	✔	✔
Between and *Among*			✔	✔		
From and *Off*			✔			
Adjectival Phrases			✔			
Adverbial Phrases			✔			
Coordinate Conjunctions			✔			
Words Used as Prepositions and Adverbs				✔	✔	✔
At and *To*				✔		
Beside and *Besides, In* and *Into*				✔		
Coordinate and Correlative Conjunctions					✔	

	C	D	E	F	G	H
Conjunctive Adverbs					✔	
Subordinate Conjunctions					✔	✔
Without and *Unless, Like, As,* and *As If*					✔	✔
PHRASES, CLAUSES	C	D	E	F	G	H
Adjectival Phrases				✔	✔	
Adverbial Phrases				✔	✔	
Adjectival Clauses					✔	✔
Adverbial Clauses					✔	✔
Restrictive and Nonrestrictive Clauses					✔	
Noun Clauses						✔
PARTICIPLES, GERUNDS, INFINITIVES	C	D	E	F	G	H
Participles						✔
Dangling Participles						✔
Gerunds						✔
Infinitives						✔
Hidden and Split Infinitives						✔
WORD STUDY SKILLS	C	D	E	F	G	H
Synonyms	✔	✔	✔	✔		
Antonyms	✔	✔				
Homophones	✔	✔	✔			
Contractions	✔	✔				
Compound Words		✔				

Correlation of Grade 6 *Voyages in English, 2006,* and Level F *Exercises in English, 2008*

Exercises in English, 2008

- Grammar is arranged in the same order as in *Voyages*, 2006, allowing students to work through the books simultaneously.

- Each grammar section in *Voyages* is supported by at least one lesson in *Exercises*.

- Some grammar sections in *Voyages* are supported by two or more lessons in *Exercises*. For example, Section 1.6 of *Voyages*, Grade 6, treats nouns used as objects. This section is supported by three lessons in *Exercises* that treat separately nouns used as direct objects, nouns used as indirect objects, and nouns used as objects of prepositions. This gives students extra practice in discrete grammar points.

- The grammar explanations in *Exercises* were rewritten to match those in *Voyages*, making it easy to move back and forth between books.

- An entire chapter of diagramming was added to *Exercises* to match that in *Voyages*. (This replaces the old Research Skills section. Research skills are taught in *Voyages* as part of the writing process, not as part of the grammar.)

- The Handbook of Terms for each level was rewritten to match that of *Voyages*.

- The TE front matter now contains a correlation of *Exercises* with the appropriate grade level of *Voyages*. (This replaces the old Sentence Analysis section.)

Features that were retained from the old *Exercises* include:

- Each exercise is based on grade-level science, social studies, or language arts content.

- The items in each exercise are divisible by 5 for easy grading.

- Character education lessons appear throughout each book.

- Section reviews provide regular assessment.

- Writing in context and self-assessment allow students to practice what they learn and to evaluate their own work.

- The TE contains overprinted answers.

- The TE front matter contains a scope and sequence chart of the entire program.

EXERCISES in ENGLISH

LEVEL
F

LOYOLAPRESS.

CHICAGO

Consultants

Therese Elizabeth Bauer
Martina Anne Erdlen
Anita Patrick Gallagher
Patricia Healey
Irene Kervick
Susan Platt

Linguistics Advisor

Timothy G. Collins
National-Louis University

Series Design: Loyola Press
Interior Art:
Jim Mitchell: 2, 19, 21, 42, 63, 87, 104, 109, 126.
Greg Phillips: 12, 51, 78, 80, 136.
All interior illustrations not listed above are by Mona Mark/Represented by Anita Grien.

ISBN-10: 0-8294-2344-3; ISBN-13: 978-0-8294-2344-0

ISBN-10: 0-8294-2338-9; ISBN-13: 978-0-8294-2338-9

Exercises in English® is a registered trademark of Loyola Press.

Manufactured in the United States of America.

06 07 08 09 10 11 12 VonH 10 9 8 7 6 5 4 3 2 1
06 07 08 09 10 11 12 VonH 10 9 8 7 6 5 4 3 2 1

Table of Contents

Name _____

1. Singular Nouns and Plural Nouns

> A noun is a name word. A **singular noun** names one person, place, or thing. A **plural noun** names more than one person, place, or thing. Add *-s* to form the plurals of most nouns. Add *-es* to form the plurals of most nouns ending in *s, x, z, ch,* or *sh.* Some plural nouns are not formed by adding *-s* or *-es.* Check a dictionary if you are not sure of a plural form.
>
> | SINGULAR | PLURAL | | SINGULAR | PLURAL |
> |----------|--------|--|----------|--------|
> | **boat** | **boats** | | **fox** | **foxes** |
> | **man** | **men** | | **fish** | **fish** |

A. Write the plural form of each word.

1. batch _____[batches]_____
2. cow _____[cows]_____
3. moose _____[moose]_____
4. bush _____[bushes]_____
5. tooth _____[teeth]_____
6. princess _____[princesses]_____
7. foot _____[feet]_____
8. ditch _____[ditches]_____
9. woman _____[women]_____
10. mile _____[miles]_____

11. computer _____[computers]_____
12. compass _____[compasses]_____
13. house _____[houses]_____
14. trout _____[trout]_____
15. series _____[series]_____
16. ox _____[oxen]_____
17. rabbit _____[rabbits]_____
18. mouse _____[mice]_____
19. book _____[books]_____
20. tax _____[taxes]_____

B. Complete each sentence with the plural form of the noun.

piece 1. Pack both _____[pieces]_____ of watermelon into the cooler.

child 2. Many _____[children]_____ begin their education in preschool.

box 3. How many moving _____[boxes]_____ did your family buy?

sheep 4. We saw six _____[sheep]_____ at the fair.

refugee 5. The _____[refugees]_____ fled to a neighboring country.

2. More Singular Nouns and Plural Nouns

If a noun ends in *y* preceded by a vowel, form the plural by adding *-s.* If a noun ends in *y* preceded by a consonant, change the *y* to *i* and add *-es.*

SINGULAR	PLURAL	SINGULAR	PLURAL
valley	**valleys**	**colony**	**colonies**

If a noun ends in *o* preceded by a vowel, form the plural by adding *-s.* If a noun ends in *o* preceded by a consonant, form the plural by adding *-es.* There are exceptions to this rule, so consult a dictionary to be sure.

SINGULAR	PLURAL	SINGULAR	PLURAL
radio	**radios**	**tomato**	**tomatoes**
video	**videos**	**taco**	**tacos**

For most nouns ending in *f* or *fe,* form the plurals by adding *-s.* For some nouns ending in *f* or *fe,* change the *f* or *fe* to *ves.* Check a dictionary if necessary.

SINGULAR	PLURAL	SINGULAR	PLURAL
roof	**roofs**	**leaf**	**leaves**

Complete each sentence with the plural form of the noun.

inventor 1. Thomas Edison is one of America's most important ____[inventors]____.

life 2. His inventions changed people's ____[lives]____.

assistant 3. Edison had a team of ____[assistants]____.

supply 4. He provided the ____[supplies]____ they needed to work.

movie 5. Edison invented the cameras, film, and projectors that made ____[movies]____ possible.

battery 6. He also developed a better way to make ____[batteries]____.

factory 7. Edison designed and built many kinds of ____[factories]____.

torpedo 8. During World War I, he helped the U.S. military forces build ____[torpedoes]____.

key 9. One of the ____[keys]____ to Edison's success was reading. Before he began a project, he read a lot about the subject.

day 10. Three ____[days]____ after Edison died, much of America dimmed its lights for one minute in his honor.

Thomas Edison always read as much as he could before he started a new project. Give an example of a way you can use reading to help yourself.

Name _____

3. Count Nouns and Noncount Nouns

> **Count nouns** name things that can be counted. Count nouns have singular and plural forms. **Noncount nouns** name things that cannot be counted. Noncount nouns do not have plural forms.
>
> | COUNT | NONCOUNT | COUNT | NONCOUNT |
> |---|---|---|---|
> | suitcases | luggage | chairs | furniture |
> | lemons | lemonade | emotions | anger |
>
> Some nouns can be count or noncount.
> **He baked two pies.** (count)   **He had pie for dessert.** (noncount)

A. Circle each count noun. Underline each noncount noun.

1. The ancient (Aztecs) inhabited what is now Mexico.
2. (Farmers) in the (highlands) grew corn.
3. They traded their grain for (things) from the (lowlands.)
4. (Artisans) made jewelry out of gold and silver.
5. (Potters) made beautiful (jars) out of clay.
6. The (Aztecs) did not have an (alphabet.)
7. They used (pictographs) to write (stories.)
8. The (Aztecs) studied the (sun,) the (moon,) and the (stars.)
9. They developed a (calendar) based on these (bodies.)
10. Their (calendar) had 365 (days) in a (year.)
11. The (people) planted (gardens) on (islands) made of mud.
12. (Trees) were planted to hold the soil together.
13. The (Aztecs) built magnificent (temples) in honor of their (gods.)
14. The (temples) were in the (shape) of (pyramids.)
15. (People) today show admiration for these (accomplishments.)

B. Complete each sentence with a noun. Write **C** if it is a count noun or **N** if it is a noncount noun. [Answers will vary. Sample answers are given.]

__[N]__ 1. Farmers in my state raise _____[corn]_____ .

__[C]__ 2. A factory near here manufactures _____[air conditioners]_____ .

__[N]__ 3. I often buy _____[bread]_____ at the supermarket.

__[N]__ 4. I can make _____[noise]_____ if I want to.

__[C]__ 5. I like to eat _____[carrots]_____ .

4. Concrete Nouns and Abstract Nouns

> A **concrete noun** names a thing that can be seen or touched.
>
> **The Greek <u>temple</u> is at the top of a <u>mountain</u>.**
>
> An **abstract noun** expresses a quality or a condition. It names something that cannot be seen or touched. Abstract nouns can be formed from other words by adding suffixes such as *-dom*, *-hood*, *-ion*, *-tion*, *-ity*, *-ment*, *-ness*, *-ry*, *-ship*, *-th*, and *-ty*.
>
> **<u>Democracy</u> had its <u>origin</u> in ancient Greece.**

A. Underline the concrete nouns in each sentence.
Circle the abstract nouns.

1. <u>People</u> in ancient (times) had differing (values) and (beliefs.)

2. Some Greek (kingdoms) valued (toughness) and (discipline.)

3. All (authority) in these (governments) was held by the <u>king</u>.

4. The <u>army</u> was extremely important in keeping (order.)

5. <u>Slaves</u> and <u>peasants</u> farmed the <u>land</u> and had few (rights.)

6. Other Greek (societies) believed in (freedom) and (democracy.)

7. They valued (truth,) (beauty,) and (order.)

8. Their <u>citizens</u> erected beautiful <u>buildings</u> and <u>statues</u>.

9. <u>Plato</u>, a Greek <u>philosopher</u>, wrote about democratic (principles.)

10. His most famous <u>book</u> is *The Republic*.

B. Write an abstract noun for each word by adding a suffix.
[Possible answers are given.]

1. good _____ [goodness] _____

2. brave _____ [bravery] _____

3. friend _____ [friendship] _____

4. king _____ [kingdom, kingship] _____

5. grow _____ [growth] _____

6. leader _____ [leadership] _____

7. entertain _____ [entertainment] _____

8. appreciate _____ [appreciation] _____

9. accomplish _____ [accomplishment] _____

10. honest _____ [honesty] _____

Name _____

5. Nouns Used as Subjects

A noun can be the subject of a verb. The **subject** tells what the sentence is **about**.

The Trojan War, fought by two ancient city-states, is the subject of a famous legend.

During the war Greek <u>soldiers</u> from Sparta attacked Troy.

A. Underline the subject in each sentence.

1. <u>Menelaus</u> was the king of Sparta.

2. His wife's <u>name</u> was Helen.

3. His <u>wife</u> fell in love with a prince from Troy and followed him there.

4. According to legend, the <u>Greeks</u> started a war against Troy.

5. The <u>war</u> lasted more than 11 years.

6. Finally, a Greek <u>soldier</u> suggested a tactic.

7. His <u>plan</u> was to build a large wooden statue of a horse.

8. Greek <u>soldiers</u> hid inside the horse.

9. The Greek <u>army</u> left the horse near the gates of Troy and sailed away.

10. The <u>people</u> found the statue and took it into the city.

11. A <u>woman</u> of Troy tried to warn the people about the statue.

12. Cassandra's <u>warnings</u> were ignored.

13. The <u>ships</u> carrying the Greeks returned that night.

14. The <u>troops</u> inside the horse emerged and opened the city gates.

15. <u>Troy</u> lost the war because of this surprise attack by the Greeks.

B. Use each noun as the subject of a sentence. [Sentences will vary. Sample answers are given.]

1. Greece _____ [Greece is surrounded by three seas.] _____

2. Troy _____ [Troy was the site of the Trojan War.] _____

3. legend _____ [The legend of the Trojan War was based on many ancient stories.] _____

4. Cassandra _____ [Cassandra had the ability to see into the future.] _____

5. the Trojan horse _____ [The Trojan horse gave the Greeks a way to win the war.] _____

6. Nouns Used as Subject Complements

> A noun can be used as a subject complement. A **subject complement** is a noun that completes the meaning of a linking verb in a sentence. It renames or describes the subject. The most common linking verbs are forms of the verb *be* (*is, am, are, was, were,* and so on).
>
> **Japan is a country in Asia.** (country = Japan)

A. Underline each subject complement.

1. Japan is a country of islands.

2. Korea, China, and Russia are the nearest neighbors of Japan.

3. The capital of Japan is Tokyo.

4. Tokyo is a large, densely populated city.

5. The official language of the country is Japanese.

6. In the Japanese language the name of the country is not Japan.

7. The name in Japanese is Nippon.

8. Of Japan's four major islands, the biggest is Honshu.

9. Many of the Japanese people are farmers and fishers.

10. Rice is an important crop in Japan.

11. Fish, both fresh and canned, is an important product.

12. Japan, however, is not primarily an agricultural country.

13. Japan is a major industrial country.

14. It is a notable producer of cars, electronics, and machines.

15. In fact, Japan is a major economic power.

B. Circle the subject in each sentence. Underline the subject complement.

1. Japan is a mountainous country.

2. Some of its mountains are volcanoes.

3. The most famous volcano in Japan is Mount Fuji.

4. This mountain is the subject of many works of art.

5. A climb to the top of Mount Fuji is an important goal of many Japanese.

7. Nouns Used as Direct Objects

A noun can be used as the direct object of a verb. A **direct object** answers the question *whom* or *what* after the verb.

VERB   DIRECT OBJECT   VERB   DIRECT OBJECT

Britain acquired Hong Kong in the 1800s. It ruled the colony until 1997.

A. Circle the direct object(s) in each sentence. The verbs are *italicized*.

1. Hong Kong *includes* some 200 islands off the south coast of China.

2. Britain *leased* this territory from China in 1898.

3. Hong Kong *reclaimed* land from the sea to gain more space.

4. Hong Kong *traded* goods with the rest of China until 1949.

5. At that time Britain *forbade* trade with Communist China.

6. Since the 1960s Hong Kong *has manufactured* many goods for trade.

7. For more than 30 years China *requested* the return of Hong Kong.

8. Britain officially *returned* the land to China on July 1, 1997.

9. Now the People's Republic of China *governs* Hong Kong.

10. By Chinese law Hong Kong *will have* a capitalist economy for several decades.

B. Underline the verb in each sentence. Circle each direct object.

1. An emperor of China, Qin Shi Huang, began the Great Wall in 221 BC.

2. The builders used brick, stone, and soil for the wall.

3. The wall protected the country's border.

4. It kept enemies out of China.

5. Guards on the wall built fires.

6. Smoke from a fire warned people about enemies in the area.

7. Through the use of satellites, scientists studied the wall.

8. With the satellite data they discovered more sections below ground.

9. The Chinese government has plans for wall repairs as necessary.

10. Today the wall amazes tourists from all over the world.

8. Nouns Used as Indirect Objects

Nouns

> A noun can be used as the indirect object of a verb. An **indirect object** tells *to whom, for whom, to what,* or *for what* the action was done.
>
> | VERB | INDIRECT OBJECT | DIRECT OBJECT |
> |------|-----------------|---------------|
> | **Iris taught** | **the old dog** | **new tricks.** |

A. Underline the verb in each sentence. Circle the indirect object. The direct object is *italicized*.

1. The hospital volunteer read the (patient) a *story*.
2. The school committee awarded (Marjorie) a *prize* for her essay.
3. Mrs. Jones bought her (son) a new *bicycle*.
4. I sent the (editor) a *letter* about a new park for our neighborhood.
5. The museum offered the (owner) a million *dollars* for the painting.
6. The soloist sang the (audience) a beautiful *ballad*.
7. Mrs. Williamson told the (children) a *story* about visiting the Kremlin.
8. The music teacher taught the (class) a patriotic *song*.
9. George Washington told (people) the *truth*.
10. Tyrone gave his (mother) some *roses* on Mother's Day.

B. Complete each sentence with a noun used as an indirect object. Underline the direct object. [Sample answers are given.]

1. The teacher gave _____[the students]_____ their homework assignment.
2. The U.S. Constitution guarantees _____[people]_____ the right to vote.
3. The movie star sent _____[the fan]_____ an autographed picture.
4. Their father promised _____[the children]_____ pizza for dinner.
5. Ms. Gibbs was pleased with the service at the hotel, so she wrote _____[the manager]_____ a complimentary letter.
6. The press secretary handed _____[the reporter]_____ a copy of the president's speech.
7. Mr. Glass sent _____[the bookstore owner]_____ an order for 10 books.
8. The instructor taught _____[the student]_____ the rules of the road.
9. The guide showed _____[the tourists]_____ the desk where the president worked.
10. The usher offered _____[the patron]_____ a program with information about the play.

9. Nouns Used as Objects of Prepositions

> A noun can be used as the object of a preposition. Prepositions show time, direction, place, and relationship. Some common prepositions are *in, into, on, to, by, for, from, at, with,* and *without.* The noun that follows a preposition in a prepositional phrase is called the **object of the preposition**; it answers *whom* or *what* after the preposition.
>
> | PREPOSITION | OBJECT | PREPOSITION | OBJECT |
> |---|---|---|---|
> | Venice is located <u>on</u> | islands | that are in the | Adriatic Sea. |

A. Circle each object of a preposition. The prepositions are *italicized.*

1. Venice is a city *in* Italy, a country *of* southern Europe.
2. Venice was an important port *during* the Middle Ages.
3. Venetian merchants traded *with* many different countries.
4. Venetian ships traveled *between* Italy and the Middle East.
5. Marco Polo, the famous explorer *of* China, was *from* Venice.
6. Today Venice is famous *for* beautiful buildings.
7. The Rialto Bridge passes *over* the Grand Canal *in* the center *of* the city.
8. Cars cannot be driven *into* Venice, so *outside* the city are parking lots.
9. People travel *through* the city *on* vaporettos, which are water buses.
10. Tourists ride *in* gondolas, small boats paddled *by* large oars.

B. Complete each sentence with prepositions. [Possible answers are shown.]

1. _____[In]_____ 1271 Marco Polo traveled _____[to]_____ China.
2. _____[On]_____ the trip he passed _____[through]_____ Turkey, Iran, and Afghanistan.
3. His party traveled _____[by]_____ boat, _____[on]_____ foot, and _____[on]_____ camels.
4. Marco Polo stayed _____[in]_____ China _____[for]_____ 17 years.
5. He met people _____[in]_____ China, India, Mongolia, and other countries.
6. He worked _____[for]_____ the emperor _____[of]_____ China, Kublai Khan.
7. After returning _____[to]_____ Italy, he wrote a book _____[about]_____ the trip.
8. Many people _____[in]_____ Italy didn't believe his amazing stories _____[about]_____ China.
9. Marco Polo's book has been translated _____[into]_____ many languages.
10. He may be the most famous traveler _____[in]_____ the history _____[of]_____ the world!

9

10. Possessive Nouns

A **possessive noun** expresses possession or ownership. The singular possessive is formed by adding -'s after the singular noun. The plural possessive is formed by adding an apostrophe after the final s of a regular plural noun or by adding -'s after an irregular plural noun.

A. For each noun write these forms: singular possessive, plural, and plural possessive. Use a dictionary if necessary.

	SINGULAR POSSESSIVE	PLURAL	PLURAL POSSESSIVE
1. turkey	[turkey's]	[turkeys]	[turkeys']
2. neighbor	[neighbor's]	[neighbors]	[neighbors']
3. driver	[driver's]	[drivers]	[drivers']
4. sheep	[sheep's]	[sheep]	[sheep's]
5. child	[child's]	[children]	[children's]
6. fox	[fox's]	[foxes]	[foxes']
7. teacher	[teacher's]	[teachers]	[teachers']
8. woman	[woman's]	[women]	[women's]
9. man	[man's]	[men]	[men's]
10. sister-in-law	[sister-in-law's]	[sisters-in-law]	[sisters-in-law's]

B. Rewrite each phrase, using a possessive noun.

1. the orders of the coach   [the coach's orders]

2. a delay of an hour   [an hour's delay]

3. the home of my parents   [my parents' home]

4. the books of the teacher   [the teacher's books]

5. the toys of the children   [the children's toys]

11. More Possessive Nouns

Notice how the singular and plural possessives are formed.

	SINGULAR	PLURAL
REGULAR	**student's desk**	**students' desks**
IRREGULAR	**man's car**	**men's cars**

A. Complete each sentence with the possessive form of the noun.

pilot   1. A _____[pilot's]_____ training requires long hours of hard study.

Sally   2. _____[Sally's]_____ running shoes are in the upstairs closet.

soldiers   3. We listened to the rhythmic sound of the _____[soldiers']_____ feet as the group marched.

Mrs. Riddle   4. Tina and Sue washed _____[Mrs. Riddle's]_____ car.

boys   5. The _____[boys']_____ books are in their backpacks.

women   6. _____[Women's]_____ coats are on sale this week.

Thomas   7. Did you find _____[Thomas's]_____ in-line skates?

brother-in-law   8. On Thanksgiving Day we tasted my _____[brother-in-law's]_____ special sweet potatoes.

deer   9. The _____[deer's]_____ large antlers show that it is quite old.

guards   10. The security _____[guards']_____ office is near the exit.

B. Rewrite each phrase, using a possessive noun.

1. the request of the librarian _____[the librarian's request]_____

2. the work of three scientists _____[the scientists' work]_____

3. the diagnosis of the doctor _____[the doctor's diagnosis]_____

4. the bicycles of the girls _____[the girls' bicycles]_____

5. the cell phones of the workers _____[the workers' cell phones]_____

6. the shouts of our children _____[our children's shouts]_____

7. a pen of Mr. James _____[Mr. James's pen]_____

8. the red feathers of the cardinals _____[the cardinals' red feathers]_____

9. the statements of some witnesses _____[some witnesses' statements]_____

10. the suitcases of my guests _____[my guests' suitcases]_____

Nouns

12. Nouns Showing Separate and Joint Possession

Separate possession occurs when two or more people own things independently. **Joint possession** occurs when two or more people own something together. To show separate possession, use -'s after each noun. To show joint possession, use -'s after the last noun only.

> **Carl and Peter each did a project. Carl's and Peter's projects are completed.**
>
> **Mary and Lisa did a project together. Mary and Lisa's project is completed.**

A. Read each sentence. On the line write **S** if separate possession is shown or **J** if joint possession is shown.

____[J]____ 1. Jim and Karen's project was a model of an Aztec pyramid.

____[S]____ 2. Laura's and Tom's projects are on the table in the hall.

____[J]____ 3. Ken and Susan's report is on Benjamin Franklin.

____[J]____ 4. Leo and Pablo's assignment was a map of the Oregon Trail.

____[S]____ 5. Lou's and Marta's presentations were excellent.

B. Read each pair of sentences. Combine each pair into a single sentence that shows separate or joint possession. [Sentences may vary.]

1. Ron and Ella have a poodle. It won the dog show.

   [Ron and Ella's poodle won the dog show.] _____

2. Misha and Harriet each have a dachshund. They were the friendliest dogs in the show.

   [Misha's and Harriet's dachshunds were the friendliest dogs in the show.] _____

3. That Labrador retriever belongs to Chris and Jason. It won Best of Breed.

   [Chris and Jason's Labrador retriever won Best of Breed.] _____

4. Elizabeth and Matt each had a cocker spaniel. Those dogs were playful.

   [Elizabeth's and Matt's cocker spaniels were playful.] _____

5. Allison and Nicole each brought a beagle. The dogs chewed on their toys.

   [Allison's and Nicole's beagles chewed on their toys.] _____

13. Appositives

An **appositive** is a word that follows a noun. It renames the noun or explains its meaning. An **appositive phrase** is an appositive and its modifiers. A **nonrestrictive** appositive or appositive phrase is not essential to the meaning of the sentence. It is set off by commas. A **restrictive** appositive or appositive phrase is necessary to the meaning of a sentence. It is not set off by commas.

NONRESTRICTIVE **The American flag, a symbol of our country, is red, white, and blue.**
(The appositive is not necessary to know what color the flag is.)

RESTRICTIVE **The seamstress Betsy Ross is said to have made the first flag.**
(The appositive is necessary to know who the seamstress was.)

Circle each noun used as an appositive. Underline the noun(s) it renames or describes. On the line write **N** if the appositive is nonrestrictive or **R** if it is restrictive.

___[N]___ 1. The Continental Congress, a group of American patriots, played a key role in America's fight for independence.

___[R]___ 2. The Philadelphia patriot Thomas Paine wrote *Common Sense*.

___[R]___ 3. The Boston politician Samuel Adams opposed the British tax on tea.

___[N]___ 4. Thomas Jefferson, a patriot from Virginia, wrote much of the Declaration of Independence.

___[N]___ 5. John Hancock, the president of the Continental Congress, was the first signer of the Declaration of Independence.

___[R]___ 6. The printer and inventor Benjamin Franklin also signed the document.

___[N]___ 7. George III, the king of England, sent troops to the colonies.

___[N]___ 8. The Battle of Lexington, the first armed fight of the American Revolution, took place on April 19, 1775.

___[N]___ 9. George Washington, the first president of the United States, had commanded an army during the Revolutionary War.

___[R]___ 10. The Polish officer Casimir Pulaski fought at the Battle of Brandywine.

___[R]___ 11. The French aristocrat the Marquis de Lafayette also traveled to America to help the colonists.

___[R]___ 12. The silversmith Paul Revere warned the people that British troops were going to attack soon.

___[N]___ 13. The Redcoats, the British soldiers, could not defeat the colonists.

___[R]___ 14. The British leader General Cornwallis lost several battles.

___[N]___ 15. Yorktown, the last important battle of the war, was won by the Americans.

14. More Appositives

A subject, a subject complement, a direct object, an indirect object, or an object of a preposition can have an appositive.

Thomas Jefferson, a lawyer, held many public offices.
Jefferson became minister to France, the successor of Benjamin Franklin.
He designed his own home, Monticello.
The Continental Congress gave Thomas Jefferson, a good writer, the job of drafting a declaration of independence.
I am reading about Thomas Jefferson, our third president.

Underline each appositive. Circle the noun it explains.

1. Thomas Jefferson studied at the (College of William and Mary,) a school in Virginia.

2. He was appointed to the (Second Continental Congress,) the colonies' government, in 1775.

3. In 1776 Jefferson wrote the (Declaration of Independence,) a key document of American history.

4. The Declaration of Independence contained a long list of complaints about (George III,) the king of England.

5. In 1784 Jefferson agreed to succeed the U.S. (ambassador) to France, Benjamin Franklin.

6. Because Jefferson did not like to speak in public, as president he gave only two (speeches,) his inaugural addresses.

7. He even made the State of the Union (address,) the president's annual report to Congress, in writing.

8. Usually he did not meet in person with the (cabinet,) his political advisors.

9. Cabinet members sent him (memos,) summaries of their recommendations.

10. The (Louisiana Purchase,) the most important event in his presidency, took place in 1803.

11. Jefferson bought the territory from (Napoleon,) the leader of France.

12. Jefferson paid a low (price,) only $15 million dollars, for the entire territory.

13. Jefferson ordered his private (secretary,) Meriwether Lewis, to explore the new land.

14. After he left the presidency, Jefferson turned his attention to another (interest,) architecture.

15. Jefferson designed two new (projects,) the campus of the University of Virginia and a house in Bedford, Virginia.

15. Words Used as Nouns and as Verbs

A noun is a naming word. A verb expresses action or being.
Many words can be used both as nouns and as verbs.

NOUN

The study of planets reveals surprising facts.

VERB

Scientists study the planets.

A. Above each *italicized* word write **N** if
the word is a noun or **V** if it is a verb.

[N]
1. The *rings* of Saturn are beautiful.

[V]
2. What material actually *rings* the planet?

[V]
3. Pieces of ice *form* the rings.

[V]
4. Some pieces are tiny ice particles, while others *reach* the size of icebergs.

[N]
5. In 1655 a Dutch astronomer first saw these round *forms* around Saturn.

[V]
6. Whenever possible, space probes *photograph* the rings up close.

[N]
7. Space probes can get close *views* of planets.

[V]
8. With telescopes, scientists could *view* only a few of Saturn's rings.

[N]
9. The *photographs* showed many rings around Saturn.

[N]
10. Space probes' photographs were a *surprise* to scientists.

[V]
11. What could *cause* Saturn's rings?

[N]
12. The *cause* may have been an explosion of one of Saturn's moons.

[V]
13. Forces slowly *pull* the ice in the rings down toward Saturn.

[N]
14. The *pull* of gravity is one of these forces.

[V]
15. New discoveries about planets may *surprise* scientists—and us—in the future.

B. Use each word in a sentence as a noun or a verb. The part of speech is indicated.
[Sentences will vary.]

1. study (noun) _____ [The study of plants is called botany.] _____

2. surprise (verb) _____ [Did that grade surprise you?] _____

3. photograph (noun) _____ [The child's photograph appeared in the newspaper.] ___

4. cause (verb) _____ [Carelessness can cause accidents.] _____

5. view (noun) _____ [The classroom provides a view of the football field.] ___

Nouns

16. Words Used as Nouns and as Adjectives

A noun is a naming word. An adjective describes a noun. Some words can be used as nouns and as adjectives.

NOUN	ADJECTIVE	NOUN MODIFIED
A <u>bat</u> is a mammal.	Large <u>bat</u>	<u>colonies</u> are found in caves.

Above each *italicized* word, write **A** if it is used as an adjective or **N** if it is used as a noun.

1. Many people are scared of bats, but bats do a great deal of *good*. [N]

2. For example, bats eat *insect* pests. [A]

3. In one hour a bat can eat between 600 and 1,000 *insects*. [N]

4. Therefore, bats are *good* for humans because they eliminate harmful insects. [A]

5. They are also important to some *plants*. [N]

6. Many *plant* species depend on bats for pollination. [A]

7. Bats often live in a *cave*. [N]

8. Bats may sleep in large groups, hanging from the *cave* ceiling. [A]

9. Some bats spend the *winter* months in caves. [A]

10. These bats sleep, or hibernate, during the *winter*. [N]

11. Bats are primarily *night* animals. [A]

12. They look for food during the *night* and sleep during the day. [N]

13. Bats use *sound* to guide their movements. [N]

14. The bats' *sound* emissions return to them as echoes, which enable the bats to detect objects ahead. [A]

15. The bones in a bat's wing are similar to the bones in a human *finger*. [N]

16. But the bat's *finger* bones are quite long. [A]

17. Bats' large wings are covered with *membranes*. [N]

18. The *membrane* structures of the wings allow bats to scoop insects in flight. [A]

19. *Migration* for the winter is characteristic of some bats, as it is for birds. [N]

20. Some of these *migration* flights take the bats from Mexico to the United States. [A]

17. Reviewing Nouns

A. Identify the *italicized* nouns. In Column 1 write **C** if the noun is a count noun or **N** if it is a noncount noun. In Column 2 write **A** if the noun is an abstract noun or **C** if it is a concrete noun.

	COLUMN 1	COLUMN 2
1. Japan is a *democracy*.	[C]	[A]
2. *Rice* is a staple of the Japanese diet.	[N]	[C]
3. Japan has a large *fleet* of modern fishing boats.	[C]	[C]
4. Many *automobiles* are imported from Japan.	[C]	[C]
5. *Respect* for the elderly is an important Japanese value.	[N]	[A]

B. Write the singular possessive and the plural possessive forms of each word.

	SINGULAR POSSESSIVE	PLURAL POSSESSIVE
6. country	[country's]	[countries']
7. child	[child's]	[children's]
8. citizen	[citizen's]	[citizens']
9. sheep	[sheep's]	[sheep's]
10. emperor	[emperor's]	[emperors']

C. On the line write how each *italicized* noun is used. Use the key below.

SUBJECT	SUBJECT COMPLEMENT	APPOSITIVE
S	**SC**	**A**

___[SC]___ 11. Tokyo is the *capital* of Japan.

___[A]___ 12. Sapporo, a large *city* in northern Japan, is a popular resort for skiers.

___[S]___ 13. Every day speedy bullet *trains* cross Japan.

CONTINUED

____[SC]____ 14. The emperor of Japan is the *head* of state in name only.

____[S]____ 15. The *prime minister* is the actual head of the government.

D. On the line write how each *italicized* noun is used. Use the key below.

DIRECT OBJECT	INDIRECT OBJECT	SUBJECT COMPLEMENT	APPOSITIVE
DO	**IO**	**SC**	**A**

____[SC]____ 16. Fables are short *stories* that illustrate a lesson.

____[A]____ 17. The ancier⁺ Greek writer *Aesop* is the author of a number of fables.

____[DO]____ 18. Aesop wrote *"The Fox and the Grapes."*

____[IO]____ 19. Many parents read their *children* fables at bedtime.

____[SC]____ 20. My favorite fable is *"The Crow and the Pitcher."*

Try It Yourself

Write three sentences about a country or a place that interests you.
Be sure that each sentence has a subject. Try to use appositives.

_____

_____

_____

_____

Check Your Own Work

Choose a selection from your writing portfolio, your journal, a work
in progress, an assignment from another class, or a letter. Revise it,
applying the skills you have reviewed. This checklist will help you.

✔ Do all the sentences have subjects?

✔ Have you used the correct forms of plurals?

✔ Have you used apostrophes correctly in possessive nouns?

✔ Have you used commas correctly with appositives?

Name _____

18. Personal Pronouns

A **pronoun** is a word that is used in place of a noun. A **personal pronoun** changes form to show who is speaking (first person); who is being spoken to (second person); or who, what, or where is being spoken about (third person). The first person personal pronouns are *I, me, mine, we, us* and *ours;* the second person pronouns are *you* and *yours;* and the third person pronouns are *he, she, it, him, her, his, hers, its, they, them* and *theirs.*

FIRST PERSON

I am reading a book about Angelina Grimké.

SECOND PERSON

Do you know who she is?

THIRD PERSON

She crusaded against slavery before the Civil War.

Underline each personal pronoun. Above each pronoun write what person it shows—**1** for first person, **2** for second person, and **3** for third person.

ANGELINA

1. [1] I learned about Angelina and Sarah Grimké; [3] they were crusaders against slavery.

2. Slavery seemed terrible to [3] them, and so [3] they wanted to help end [3] it.

3. The sisters wrote articles about slavery and published [3] them in newspapers and magazines.

4. [3] They told Southern women, "[2] You should talk to your husbands and friends about slavery. Tell [3] them that [2] you think [3] it is wrong."

5. [1] I think that [1] we owe a great deal to people like Sarah and Angelina Grimké because [3] they helped [1] us in the fight for human rights.

SARAH

Angelina and Sarah Grimké fought for the rights of others. Give an example of something you can do to help others in their struggle for human rights.

19. Number and Gender of Pronouns

> A pronoun is singular when it refers to one person, place, or thing.
> **Tom** sent an **e-mail** to his **mother**.
> **He** sent **it** to **her**.
>
> A pronoun is plural when it refers to more than one person, place, or thing.
> **Tonya and Maria** brought some **cookies**.
> **They** brought **them**.
>
> A **third person singular pronoun** can be masculine, feminine, or neuter.
> MASCULINE   FEMININE   NEUTER
> **He helped her prepare supper. I helped eat it.**

A. Underline the personal pronoun(s) in each sentence.
Above each write **S** if it is singular or **P** if it is plural.

1. My brother and [S] I love to travel.

2. Last year [P] we took a trip to London.

3. [S] It is a beautiful and historic city.

4. My brother went to see the changing of the guard,
   and [S] he took a picture of the colorful ceremony.

5. We bought fish and chips every day and ate [P] them for lunch.

B. On the line write a pronoun that could take the place of the *italicized* word(s).
On the same line identify the gender of each third person singular pronoun.
Write **M** if it is masculine, **F** if it is feminine, or **N** if it is neuter.

_____[They]_____ 1. *Susan and Sam* love to travel with their parents.

_____[They]_____ 2. *The two children* went to London last year.

_____[It, N]_____ 3. *London* is the capital of England.

_____[She, F]_____ 4. *Susan* enjoyed seeing the crown jewels at the Tower of London.

_____[He, M]_____ 5. *Sam* saw some old weapons there as well.

_____[it, N]_____ 6. They saw Big Ben and were impressed by *the huge clock*.

_____[them]_____ 7. Sam took photographs of *the Tower and Big Ben*.

_____[them]_____ 8. I got a beautiful postcard from *Susan and Sam*.

_____[We]_____ 9. The postcard read, "*Susan and I* are having a great time."

_____[us]_____ 10. They brought souvenirs for *my brother and me*.

Pronouns

20. Agreement of Pronouns and Antecedents

> The noun to which a pronoun refers is its **antecedent**. The pronoun must agree in person and number with the noun it replaces. A third person singular pronoun must also agree with its antecedent in gender.
>
> **Mohandas Karamchand Gandhi** was born in India in 1869; **he** became an international figure for freedom.
>
> **India** is in Asia, but **it** was ruled by the British.

A. Underline the pronoun that goes with each *italicized* antecedent.

1. The people of India were not happy with British *rule* and wanted it to end.

2. Gandhi had read the writings of *Henry David Thoreau* and had learned about civil disobedience from him.

3. Gandhi was an example for the Indian *people,* and he taught them nonviolent ways to oppose the British authorities.

4. When *Gandhi* spoke about independence, people cheered him.

5. *Gandhi* asked Indians to stop wearing clothes made in England, and he encouraged them to set up their own clothing industry.

B. Complete each sentence with a pronoun that refers to the *italicized* antecedent.

1. As *Gandhi* worked for independence, _____[he]_____ often fasted.

2. He used fasting to show *people* that _____[they]_____ needed to be nonviolent.

3. The Indian people loved *Gandhi* and called _____[him]_____ Mahatma, which means "great soul."

4. In 1947 the British left *India,* and _____[it]_____ became independent.

5. In 1948 *Gandhi* was murdered by a fanatic while _____[he]_____ was on his way to a prayer meeting.

Mohandas K. Gandhi used only peaceful means to achieve his goals. Give an example of some peaceful means you can use to deal with people who think differently than you do.

Name _____

21. Intensive Pronouns and Reflexive Pronouns

Reflexive pronouns and intensive pronouns end in *-self* or *-selves*. A **reflexive pronoun** is used as a direct object, an indirect object, or the object of a preposition. A reflexive pronoun usually refers back to the subject. An **intensive pronoun** is used to emphasize the preceding noun or pronoun; it is not essential to the sentence.

REFLEXIVE   **Trent sent himself a copy of the message.**
              Many inventors do not work by themselves.

INTENSIVE   **I myself made the grilled cheese sandwich.**
              I made the grilled cheese sandwich myself.

A. Underline each reflexive pronoun. Circle each intensive pronoun.

1. Alexander Graham Bell invented the telephone, but he did not do all the work by himself.

2. Bell had the help of Thomas Watson. Watson (himself) built the prototype phones from Bell's designs.

3. Bell and Watson did all the testing of the instruments by themselves.

4. Bell earned himself the title of inventor of the phone with the first voice transmission in 1876.

5. Bell's wife (herself,) Mabel Hubbard Bell, was interested in science.

6. She and her husband built themselves a large home in Canada where they could conduct their research.

7. Mabel Bell was deaf, but she set high goals for herself.

8. She was interested in developing airplanes and other flying machines, though she (herself) was never able to fly in one.

9. Alexander Graham Bell (himself) was responsible for new teaching methods and inventions to help the deaf.

10. We should remind ourselves of all the people like Bell who helped people have better lives.

B. Complete each sentence with the correct reflexive pronoun.

1. I cut _____ [myself] _____ while I was chopping onions.

2. Cats clean and groom _____ [themselves] _____ with their tongues.

3. We bought _____ [ourselves] _____ some popcorn to eat during the movie.

4. Oscar, you must do the project for the science fair by _____ [yourself] _____.

5. Marybeth taught _____ [herself] _____ the rules of chess.

Name _____

22. Pronouns as Subjects

> A personal pronoun can be used as the subject of a sentence.
> The **subject pronouns** are *I, we, you, he, she, it,* and *they.*
>
> **I saw the White House on a news report last night.**
> **It is a really beautiful building.**

Circle the correct pronoun in parentheses.

1. Jill, Mark, and (I me) prepared a report on Washington, D.C.

2. (We Us) did research on the Internet and at the library.

3. Pierre L'Enfant designed the city. (Him He) was from France.

4. The city was named for George Washington.
   (He Him) hired L'Enfant to design it.

5. The White House is the home of the president.
   (It They) has been the home of every
   American president since John Adams.

6. Thomas Jefferson entered the contest for the design of
   the White House. (Him He) did not win, however.

7. Dolley Madison was the wife of President James Madison. (She Her)
   rescued papers from the White House before the British burned it in 1814.

8. First Lady Jacqueline Kennedy made important contributions to the White House.
   (She Her) redecorated it with antiques and historic paintings.

9. The Washington Monument honors the country's first president.
   (It They) was opened to the public in 1885.

10. Members of the House of Representatives meet in the Capitol. The senators
    and (they them) form the legislative branch of the government.

11. The John F. Kennedy Center for the Performing Arts is in Washington, D.C.
    (They It) contains various theaters for concerts, drama, and opera.

12. (You Me) can visit many historical sites in Washington, D.C., including the
    White House, the Capitol, and the Smithsonian Institution.

13. My family and (I me) visited Washington, D.C., last spring.

14. (It She) is a really beautiful city, espcially during Cherry Blossom Festival.

15. What do (you me) want to see when you visit Washington, D.C.?

23. Pronouns as Subject Complements

A subject complement follows a linking verb and refers to the same person, place, or thing as the subject. The most common linking verbs are forms of the verb *be* (*is, are, was, were,* and so on). A **subject pronoun** can be used as a subject complement.

The editor of the school paper is she.

It is I who washed all the dishes.

A. Circle the correct pronoun in parentheses.

1. The assistant editors are Kristen and (she her).

2. It was (her she) who wrote the lead story in this issue of the paper.

3. It was (he him) who drew the cartoon that illustrated the story.

4. The photographers for the paper are Jason and (they them).

5. The page designers are Allison and (me I).

6. The English teachers were (they them) who suggested this special edition.

7. Principal Sharon Kent was (she her) who gave the go-ahead.

8. She told Ernesto that the person in charge would be (he him).

9. We knew that neither Charlie nor Phil would be (him he)—the copyboy.

10. The people writing the stories were (them they), the regular staff members.

11. Martha and Sue, as usual, would be (them they) who wrote the fashion stories.

12. I asked whether the entertainment editors could be (us we)—Katrina, Ann, and I.

13. Ernesto said that since I was already doing page design, the editors would probably be (they them).

14. When this special issue comes out, the students getting the first copies will be (us we) who did all the work.

15. The next group to receive copies will most likely be (they them) who gave their support and guidance.

B. Complete each sentence with a personal pronoun. Vary your choices. **[Answers will vary.]**

1. The first ones to cross the finish line were _____.

2. The student who will sing onstage is _____.

3. Are you sure the coach was _____ in the gym?

4. The winning designers were _____ who were on television.

5. Was the person in the skeleton costume _____?

24. Pronouns as Direct Objects

> A personal pronoun can be used as the direct object of a verb.
> The **object pronouns** are *me, us, you, him, her, it,* and *them.*
>
> **Julius Caesar was a ruler of Rome.**
> **His enemies killed <u>him</u> in 44 BC.**

A. Circle the correct pronoun in parentheses.

1. Julius Caesar was a leader in the Roman army.
   He joined (it him) as a young man.

2. He met a woman, Calpurnia, from a wealthy
   family and married (she her) in 59 BC.

3. The Romans had selected (he him) for
   public office 16 years earlier.

4. Caesar went to Gaul—what is now France—and conquered (it them).

5. Caesar had enemies in Rome. He defeated (they them) in 45 BC
   and took over the government.

6. As a ruler, Caesar reformed the calendar. We still use (them it)
   in a modified version today.

7. The Romans honored (he him) by naming July after him.

8. His stories about his battles survive, and people still read (them they).

9. Caesar's enemies killed (he him) on March 15, 44 BC.

10. Upon his death, Antony and Octavian succeeded (him he).

B. Use a personal pronoun to replace the word(s) in parentheses.

1. Cleopatra ruled _____[it]_____ (Egypt) from 51 to 30 BC.

2. Five years after becoming queen, Cleopatra met _____[him]_____ (Antony).

3. He fell in love with Cleopatra, and he married _____[her]_____ (Cleopatra).

4. The couple wanted more power, and this angered _____[them]_____ (the Romans).

5. Octavian went to Egypt and defeated Antony and _____[her]_____ (Cleopatra).
   The couple killed themselves.

25. Pronouns as Indirect Objects

> An object pronoun can be used as the **indirect object** in a sentence. The indirect object tells *to whom, for whom, to what,* or *for what* something is done.
>
> **The coach gave us our instructions.**

A. Circle the indirect object in each sentence.

1. Tom sent (me) an invitation to his birthday party.

2. I bought (him) a present.

3. His mom offered (us) cake and ice cream.

4. We gave (her) our thanks.

5. Several guests sang (him) the birthday song.

6. He awarded (them) prizes.

7. His dad told (us) some funny stories.

8. We paid (him) many compliments.

9. Tom's mother brought (us) our coats.

10. I'll send (her) a thank-you note tomorrow.

B. Complete each sentence with the correct form of the pronoun indicated in parentheses.

1. I sent _____[you]_____ a letter of complaint. *(second, singular)*

2. Please give _____[me]_____ an answer. *(first, singular)*

3. The reporter asked _____[her]_____ a question. *(third, singular, feminine)*

4. The government denied _____[them]_____ their rights. *(third, plural)*

5. His mother made _____[him]_____ a sandwich. *(third, singular, masculine)*

6. The teacher told _____[us]_____ a story. *(first, plural)*

7. The incident taught _____[her]_____ a lesson. *(third, singular, feminine)*

8. I think you owe _____[me]_____ an apology. *(first, singular)*

9. We found _____[it]_____ a new home. *(third, singular, neuter)*

10. His project earned _____[him]_____ a good grade. *(third, singular, masculine)*

26. Pronouns as Objects of Prepositions

An object pronoun can be used as the object of a preposition.
The teacher wanted to talk to <u>me</u> about my science fair project.

A. Circle the correct pronoun in parentheses.

1. Yesterday the coach read some basic basketball rules to (we us).

2. Paul told the joke to Luisa and (I me).

3. Mrs. Russo lives near (us we).

4. Is this orange juice for Maggie and (he him)?

5. The decorations for the party were made by (them they).

6. We sat in the theater balcony, and below (we us) was the entire choral group.

7. Sarah's mother forgot to give the message to (her she).

8. Frank spotted his best friend and quickly walked toward (him he).

9. Everybody has gone home except Chris and (he him).

10. I went to the Grand Canyon last fall and took pictures of (it she).

B. Write the correct object form of the pronoun in parentheses to complete each sentence.

1. I got a long e-mail from ____[her]____ (she).

2. Vassily stood near ____[me]____ (I) in the cafeteria line.

3. I have told this story about Mom and ____[them]____ (they) before.

4. We can't leave for the mall without ____[her]____ (she).

5. My brother Carlos loves fixing up his car. Last weekend he bought some new wheel covers for ____[it]____ (it).

6. Lee wants to work on the science project with Rita and ____[me]____ (I).

7. Everyone except ____[him]____ (he) is in school today.

8. Here is an apple for ____[you]____ (you).

9. Bea and Ann divided the cookies among the three of ____[us]____ (we).

10. He called on everyone in class except Ryan and ____[her]____ (she).

27. Possessive Pronouns

> A **possessive pronoun** shows possession or ownership. A possessive pronoun stands by itself; it does not modify a noun. A possessive pronoun does not have an apostrophe. The possessive pronouns are *mine, yours, his, hers, its, ours,* and *theirs.*
>
> **That history book is mine.**   **Yours is in your backpack.**

A. Underline the possessive pronoun(s) in each sentence.

1. That new skateboard is hers.

2. Ours is much larger, and yours is much smaller.

3. Mine is purple and green.

4. Those two skateboards must be theirs.

5. His is under the bed.

6. I can't find my bat. Please let me use yours.

7. This bat isn't mine. I think it's his.

8. Excuse me. Is this glove yours?

9. I left mine in the gym at school.

10. Luke lost a glove. This glove must be his.

B. Write on the line the possessive pronoun related to the personal pronoun in parentheses.

1. The green pencil is _____[hers]_____ (she).

2. The idea for the project was _____[theirs]_____ (they).

3. Please put your bicycle over there beside _____[ours]_____ (we).

4. The last house on the street is _____[his]_____ (he).

5. No, those apples are not _____[mine]_____ (I).

6. Are these books _____[yours]_____ (you)?

7. _____[Mine]_____ (I) has been missing for a week.

8. Find _____[yours]_____ (you) and then find _____[hers]_____ (she).

9. The prize-winning project was _____[hers]_____ (she).

10. Is this jacket _____[his]_____ (he) or _____[hers]_____ (she)?

28. Possessive Adjectives

> A **possessive adjective** expresses possession or ownership. A possessive adjective modifies a noun. The possessive adjectives are *my, our, your, his, her, its,* and *their.*
>
> **I got <u>my</u> tetanus shot yesterday.**

A. Underline the possessive adjective in each sentence.

1. <u>My</u> report is about vaccines.

2. Vaccines protect <u>our</u> bodies from many diseases.

3. Edward Jenner invented the first vaccine in 1798, and <u>his</u> work had important results.

4. <u>His</u> vaccine protected people against smallpox.

5. He studied a minor disease, cowpox, and noticed <u>its</u> effects on people.

6. After people had suffered from cowpox, <u>their</u> bodies were able to fight off smallpox.

7. Jenner had an idea: <u>his</u> idea was to inject people with cowpox bacteria.

8. Jenner's experiments were a success in the fight against smallpox, and <u>their</u> results led to the development of other vaccines.

9. Edna told me that she had done <u>her</u> report on vaccines too.

10. We found, however, that <u>our</u> reports focused on different scientists.

B. Write the correct form of the possessive adjective on the line. Use the adjective related to the pronoun in parentheses.

1. People need to do many things to protect _____[their]_____ (they) health.

2. We need to make sure that we get all _____[our]_____ (we) vaccinations.

3. When you receive a vaccine, it helps _____[your]_____ (you) body create antibodies to fight a disease.

4. Sometimes a person's body can create _____[its]_____ (it) own antibodies.

5. The vaccines fight such dangerous diseases as polio, diphtheria, and tetanus. Doctors know that these diseases and _____[their]_____ (they) effects can be serious.

Name _____

29. Possessive Adjectives and Contractions

> A possessive adjective expresses possession or ownership. A possessive adjective does not have an apostrophe. A **contraction** generally is formed by joining a personal pronoun and a verb. An apostrophe (') replaces the missing letter or letters.
>
> POSSESSIVE ADJECTIVE **Your report is on the fall of the Berlin Wall.**
>
> CONTRACTION **You're (= You are) supposed to give the report next week.**

A. Write **P** over the underlined word if it is a possessive adjective. Write **C** if it is a contraction.

1. The students studied about the Berlin Wall in [P] their social studies class.

2. [P] Its fall on November 9, 1989, marked communism's end in Germany.

3. [C] It's been interesting to study about the reuniting of East Germany and West Germany.

4. [C] They're now a single country.

5. What is [P] your opinion about the fall of the Berlin Wall?

B. Circle the correct word in parentheses.

1. The people of Poland had many of the same problems as the people of East Germany. From 1945 (their) they're) government was Communist.

2. (They're) Their) no longer under Communist rule.

3. (Their) They're) transition to democracy began in 1980.

4. In that year workers formed (their) they're) opposition trade union, Solidarity.

5. (Its) It's) leader was Lech Walesa.

6. Communists opposed the union, and (its) it's) existence was banned.

7. People supported the union, and (their) they're) support kept it alive.

8. In 1989 Poland had an economic crisis. (It's (Its) Communist leaders then decided to allow Solidarity to participate in elections.

9. Solidarity won many seats in the Polish congress; it reformed Poland's economy and gave back to the people (their) they're) freedoms.

10. The Polish people are glad that (they're) their) free to form their own government.

Name _____

30. More Contractions

A personal pronoun and a verb can be joined to form a contraction.
In a contraction an apostrophe replaces the missing letter or letters.

I'm (= I am) **writing a report on Morocco.**

We've (= We have) **never visited Morocco.**

A. Underline the contraction in each item. Write the pronoun and the verb that make up the contraction in the appropriate columns.

	PRONOUN	VERB
1. Morocco is a fascinating country. It's located in northwest Africa.	[It]	[is]
2. The head of the government is a king. He's named Muhammad VI.	[He]	[is]
3. He's been king since 1999.	[He]	[has]
4. Morocco has many mountains. They're among the tallest mountains in northern Africa.	[They]	[are]
5. Many Moroccans have moved to large cities. They've created a severe housing crisis in cities such as Casablanca and Fez.	[They]	[have]
6. Morocco was colonized by Spain and France. It's been independent since 1956.	[It]	[has]
7. Moroccans speak French and Arabic. They're mostly employed in agricultural jobs.	[They]	[are]
8. The capital is Rabat. It's a beautiful modern city located on the Atlantic Ocean.	[It]	[is]
9. I've never been to Morocco.	[I]	[have]
10. But we're going to visit Morocco next year.	[we]	[are]

B. Complete each sentence with the correct contraction.
Use the pronoun and verb at the left.

He is   1. Morocco's ruler is named Muhammad VI. _____[He's]_____ the King of Morocco.

It is   2. _____[It's]_____ on the Atlantic Ocean and the Mediterranean Sea.

It has   3. _____[It's]_____ been ruled by Spain and France.

They are   4. The people are religious. _____[They're]_____ mostly Muslims.

I am   5. _____[I'm]_____ going to write a report on Morocco for school.

31

31. Demonstrative Pronouns

Pronouns

> **Demonstrative pronouns** are used to point out things, places, and people. Use *this* and *these* to point out things that are near. Use *that* and *those* to point out things that are farther away. *This* and *that* are singular. *These* and *those* are plural.
>
> **This is my sweater.**   **That is my water bottle.**
> **These are my hiking boots.**   **Those are my jeans.**

A. Circle the demonstrative pronoun. In Column 1 write **N** for near or **F** for far. In Column 2 write **S** for singular or **P** for plural.

	COLUMN 1	COLUMN 2
1. (These) are the things we need for our camping trip.	[N]	[P]
2. (That) is the tent we'll take.	[F]	[S]
3. Whose sunglasses are (these?)	[N]	[P]
4. (This) is good bug repellant.	[N]	[S]
5. (That) is Dad's flashlight.	[F]	[S]
6. (Those) are the wrong batteries.	[F]	[P]
7. We need candles. Please pack (these.)	[N]	[P]
8. Whose guidebook is (this?)	[N]	[S]
9. Is (that) your sleeping bag?	[F]	[S]
10. Are (those) the inflatable pillows?	[F]	[P]

B. Complete each sentence with a demonstrative pronoun. Use the directions in parentheses.

1. Are ___[those]___ the supplies for the art project? (far)

2. ___[These]___ are not the correct markers. (near)

3. Is ___[this]___ your canvas? (near)

4. ___[These]___ are my watercolors. (near)

5. ___[That]___ is a box of felt scraps. (far)

6. Whose wooden pegs are ___[those]___? (far)

7. ___[This]___ is the glue gun I need. (near)

8. Can you drill a hole with ___[that]___? (far)

9. I need some washers. Please hand me ___[those]___. (far)

10. Is ___[this]___ the tool you need? (near)

32. Interrogative Pronouns

> An **interrogative pronoun** is used to ask a question. The interrogative pronouns are *who, whom, which, what,* and *whose.*
>
> **What is the name of the spacecraft that flew to Mars?**
>
> The interrogative pronoun *who* is used when the pronoun refers to a person and when it is the subject of a question.
>
> **Who was the first person to walk on the Moon?**
>
> The interrogative pronoun *whom* is used when the pronoun refers to a person and when it is the direct object or the indirect object of a verb or the object of a preposition.
>
> **Whom did the United States have as its first female commander of a space flight?**

A. Underline the interrogative pronoun in each sentence.
Write whether it refers to a person or a thing.

_____[person]_____ 1. <u>Who</u> were the first Americans to land on the Moon?

_____[thing]_____ 2. <u>What</u> did the spacecraft use as fuel?

_____[person]_____ 3. <u>Which</u> of the astronauts walked on the Moon first?

_____[person]_____ 4. <u>Who</u> called the astronauts while they were on the Moon?

_____[thing]_____ 5. <u>What</u> did the astronauts bring back from the Moon?

B. Complete each sentence with *which, what,* or *whose.*

1. _____[Which]_____ of the planets did American spacecraft visit first, Mars or Venus?

2. _____[What]_____ was the nationality of the first person to travel in space?

3. _____[Whose]_____ was the promise that the United States would explore the Moon within a decade?

4. _____[What]_____ is a cosmonaut?

5. _____[Which]_____ of these countries was the first to launch a rocket into space, the Soviet Union or the United States?

C. Complete each sentence with *who* or *whom.*

1. _____[Who]_____ is Neil Armstrong?

2. _____[Who]_____ was the first Russian to travel in space?

3. To _____[whom]_____ did the astronauts send their messages from the Moon?

4. _____[Whom]_____ did you discuss in your report, Neil Armstrong or John Glenn?

5. _____[Who]_____ was the captain of the latest *Discovery* flight?

Name _____

33. Indefinite Pronouns

An **indefinite pronoun** refers to any or all of a group of persons, places, or things. Among the indefinite pronouns are *anybody, anyone, anything, everybody, everyone, everything, nobody, no one, nothing, somebody, someone, something, both, few, each, either, many, neither, several, all,* and *some.*

> **We're studying European nations. Many are on the Mediterranean.**
>
> **Each of the countries on the Mediterranean uses it for recreation.**

A. Underline the indefinite pronoun(s) in each sentence.

1. Almost everybody in Italy speaks Italian, and almost everyone in Spain speaks Spanish.

2. These languages are among several that are based on Latin.

3. In both of the countries, people enjoy religious freedom.

4. Many of the cities have beautiful churches and museums.

5. The people are very friendly. If you get lost, anybody will help you.

6. Someone mentioned that Spain covers a larger area than Italy does.

7. Italy and Spain have one great similarity: each is located on a peninsula.

8. Neither is as large as Texas.

9. Each has a rich cultural heritage.

10. Do you want to visit either of these countries?

B. Complete each sentence with an indefinite pronoun.
[Answers may vary. Sample answers are given.]

1. _____[Both]_____ of the countries are democracies.

2. _____[Both]_____ are on the Mediterranean.

3. Do you know _____[anybody]_____ from Spain or Italy?

4. _____[None]_____ of my grandparents came from these countries.

5. What is the most interesting fact you know about _____[either]_____ of these countries?

Name _____

34. Verbs with Indefinite Pronouns

Many indefinite pronouns are singular; therefore, the verb must agree with a third person singular subject. Among the common singular indefinite pronouns are *another, each, either, much, neither, nobody, no one, nothing, one, other,* and pronouns formed with *any* and *some.* The indefinite pronouns *both, few, many, others,* and *several* are plural and take a verb that agrees with a third person plural subject.

SINGULAR   **Everybody appreciates the magnificence of gold.**

PLURAL   **Many of the objects from ancient civilizations are of gold or silver.**

Some indefinite pronouns, such as *all* or *none,* can be either singular or plural.

A. On the line write **S** if the *italicized* pronoun is singular or **P** if it is plural. Circle the correct verb.

__[S]__   1. *Everyone* (admires) admire) the beauty of gold and silver.

__[P]__   2. *Both* (has (have) been highly valued for hundreds of years.

__[S]__   3. *Neither* (is) are) found in great abundance on the earth.

__[P]__   4. *Both* of them (is (are) precious metals.

__[S]__   5. *Each* (last (lasts) a long time, but silver tends to turn black.

__[P]__   6. *Many* of the earth's metals (shine) shines), and both gold and silver have a luster.

__[S]__   7. *Either* (is) are) frequently used in jewelry designs.

__[P]__   8. *Some* of the objects in ancient tombs (is (are) gold jewelry.

__[P]__   9. *Many* of the pieces of jewelry (is (are) beautiful.

__[S]__ 10. *Nobody* (fails) fail) to admire the magnificent gold mask of the Egyptian king Tut.

B. Complete the sentences with *was* or *were.*

1. Two great gold rushes occurred in United States history.
   Both ___[were]___ during the 19th century.

2. Each ___[was]___ to a different location, California and Alaska.

3. Many of the miners ___[were]___ immigrants from Europe and Asia.

4. Everyone ___[was]___ interested in getting rich.

5. However, very few ___[were]___ lucky enough to find gold.

35. Indefinite Pronouns and Double Negatives

The indefinite pronouns *nothing, no one,* and *nobody* are negatives. When a sentence contains a negative word such as *never* or *not,* do not use a negative pronoun. Instead, use *anything, anyone,* or *anybody.*

Kevin could not read anything on the chalkboard.

Kevin could read nothing on the chalkboard.

Circle the correct indefinite pronoun in parentheses.

1. Tim didn't find (nothing (anything)) in the old trunk in the attic.

2. I'm sorry. There is ((nothing) anything) in the mailbox for you today.

3. (Anybody (Nobody)) spoke about the problem of air pollution.

4. I have never seen (no one (anyone)) as tall as Kevin Garnett!

5. Sydney broke his arm and can't carry ((anything) nothing).

6. ((Nobody) Anybody) wants to go out in this heavy downpour.

7. I found (anything (nothing)) in the parking lot except broken glass.

8. The winner was so excited that she couldn't say (nothing (anything)).

9. This week ((nobody) anybody) in our class arrived late to school.

10. Carmen hasn't eaten ((anything) nothing) since breakfast.

11. (Anybody (Nobody)) should have been in the park after dark.

12. I didn't tell the secret to ((anybody) nobody).

13. Our plan is foolproof! ((Nothing) Anything) can go wrong.

14. Doesn't ((anybody) nobody) know a good baseball Web site?

15. The detectives looked for clues, but they couldn't find (nothing (anything)).

16. The last math problem was so difficult that ((nobody) anybody) could solve it.

17. Bears live near this campground, so keep all your food in the car. Don't leave ((anything) nothing) in your tent.

18. I spent four hours at the mall, but I didn't buy ((anything) nothing).

19. There wasn't ((anything) nothing) in the refrigerator.

20. Accidents can happen to ((anyone) no one).

Pronouns

36. Reviewing Pronouns

A. Identify each *italicized* pronoun. In Column 1 write **1** for first person, **2** for second person, or **3** for third person. In Column 2 write **S** for singular or **P** for plural, and in Column 3 write **S** if the pronoun is a subject pronoun or **O** if it is an object pronoun.

	COLUMN 1	COLUMN 2	COLUMN 3
1. *We* saw a delightful movie about Joy and George Adamson, who lived in Africa for many years.	[1]	[P]	[S]
2. George was a game warden in Kenya. *He* protected animals.	[3]	[S]	[S]
3. One day a lioness attacked *him*.	[3]	[S]	[O]
4. He had to shoot *her* to save his life.	[3]	[S]	[O]
5. He found that she had three cubs, and he took *them* home.	[3]	[P]	[O]

B. On the line, write how each underlined pronoun is used. Use the key below.

SUBJECT	SUBJECT COMPLEMENT	DIRECT OBJECT	OBJECT OF PREPOSITION
S	**SC**	**DO**	**OP**

[DO] 6. The Adamsons adopted one cub. They called her Elsa.

[S] 7. She was a beautiful and lively cub.

[OP] 8. She lived with them.

[DO] 9. They raised her in their home.

[SC] 10. The lioness in Joy Adamson's book *Born Free* was she.

C. Identify each *italicized* pronoun. Use the key below.

REFLEXIVE PRONOUN	POSSESSIVE PRONOUN	INDEFINITE PRONOUN
R	**P**	**I**

[I] 11. Joy and George loved Elsa, but *each* knew that there was a problem.

[I] 12. *Neither* wanted Elsa to live with them forever.

[I] 13. *Both* wanted Elsa to have a life in the wild.

[R] 14. So Elsa had to learn the skills to survive in the wild by *herself*.

[P] 15. Joy and George taught Elsa the skills of survival so that a life in the wild could be *hers*.

CONTINUED

Pronouns

D. Circle the correct personal pronoun.

16. My friends and (me (I)) learned a lesson from the movie *Born Free.*

17. Animals have a natural habitat. ((They) Them) were born to live in it.

18. Joy raised Elsa. Elsa lived with ((her) she) until the lioness was three.

19. Elsa was able to live in the wild. ((She) Her) had cubs of her own.

20. In several books Joy tells about her experiences in Africa, and many people have enjoyed reading about (they (them).)

E. Circle the correct pronoun.

21. Are you sure there is ((no one) anyone) to (who (whom)) we can write to learn more about helping wild animals?

22. Doesn't (no one (anyone)) know ((who) whom) started the Born Free organization?

23. ((Who) Whom) hasn't found ((anything) nothing) about the group on the Web?

24. Isn't there (nobody (anyone)) ((who) whom) has observed animals in a natural setting?

25. Can't you tell us ((anything) nothing) about the person with (who (whom)) you have shared the experience?

Try It Yourself

Write four sentences about a person you admire. Tell what the person did or does. Explain why you admire him or her. Be sure to use pronouns correctly.

_____

_____

_____

_____

Check Your Own Work

Choose a selection from your writing portfolio, your journal, a work in progress, an assignment from another subject, or a letter. Revise it, applying the skills you have reviewed. This checklist will help you.

✔ Have you used subject and object pronouns correctly?

✔ Have you formed possessive pronouns and possessive adjectives correctly?

✔ Have you used interrogative pronouns in your sentences correctly?

✔ Have you avoided double negatives?

Name _____

37. Descriptive Adjectives

> **Adjectives** describe nouns. Descriptive adjectives can tell about age, size, shape, color, origin, or other qualities.
>
> The <u>large</u> painting hung near the <u>south</u> entrance of the museum.
> <u>Italian</u> artists painted on <u>wet</u> plaster to create frescos.

A. Circle each descriptive adjective. Underline the noun it describes.

1. Throughout history, people have made pictures in (different) <u>ways</u>.

2. (Early) <u>people</u> painted on the walls of caves.

3. They used (colorful) <u>pigments</u> made from soil.

4. Egyptians boiled (various) <u>plants</u> to make dyes.

5. People in Asia made (remarkable) <u>colors</u> from clay.

6. (European) <u>painters</u> in the 1300s made paints from eggs.

7. Painters today often use (acrylic) <u>paints</u>.

8. Crayons made of wax and pigment come in (bright) <u>colors</u>.

9. (Creative) <u>artists</u> sometimes use crayons to draw pictures.

10. Sculptors sometimes make (mammoth) <u>constructions</u> out of metal.

11. They may also make collages of (simple) <u>objects</u> that they find.

12. (Delicate) <u>drawings</u> can be made with pen and ink.

13. Artists today do (original) <u>work</u> with videos.

14. They use computers to adjust (digital) <u>photos</u>.

15. (Beautiful) <u>art</u> can be found almost anywhere.

B. Write an adjective to describe each noun. [Answers will vary.]

1. _____ sunset   6. _____ painting

2. _____ field   7. _____ pizza

3. _____ puppy   8. _____ skateboard

4. _____ boat   9. _____ report

5. _____ artist   10. _____ computer

38. More Descriptive Adjectives

Adjectives

> Descriptive adjectives tell about characteristics such as age, size, shape, color, taste, or origin.
>
> **In the <u>old</u> basket were <u>large</u>, <u>round</u>, <u>red</u> apples.**

A. Put each adjective in the appropriate column. Then add two adjectives of your own to each column.

circular	large	Danish	new	pink
purple	square	young	tiny	Thai

AGE	SIZE	SHAPE	COLOR	ORIGIN
[new]	[large]	[circular]	[pink]	[Danish]
[young]	[tiny]	[square]	[purple]	[Thai]

B. Complete each sentence with the correct adjective. Use the clue in parentheses for help. Use each adjective once. **[Answers may vary.]**

excellent	green	Italian	old	popular
delicious	healthful	large	orange	sweet

1. *Zucchini* is an _____[Italian]_____ *(origin)* word that means "little squash."

2. Zucchini are _____[healthful]_____ *(quality)* vegetables that are good for everyone.

3. Because zucchini are low in calories, they are an _____[excellent]_____ *(quality)* choice for dieters.

4. Cooks choose zucchini with shiny, _____[green]_____ *(color)* skins.

5. Zucchini have a delicate, almost _____[sweet]_____ *(taste)* flavor.

6. Small zucchini are usually less bland than _____[large]_____ *(size)* ones.

7. People make _____[delicious]_____ *(taste)* salads with raw zucchini.

8. It is an _____[old]_____ *(age)* custom in Italy to eat zucchini cooked with eggplant, tomatoes, and peppers.

9. Another _____[popular]_____ *(quality)* use of zucchini is in zucchini bread.

10. The bright _____[orange]_____ *(color)* and yellow zucchini flowers are also edible.

Name _____

39. Definite and Indefinite Articles

> *A, an,* and *the* are a type of adjective that points out nouns. They are
> called **articles.** *The* is a **definite article.** *A* and *an* are **indefinite articles.**
> The article *an* is used before a vowel sound.
> The article *a* is used before a consonant sound.
>
> **The tourists went to an island for a vacation.**

A. Write the correct indefinite article before each word.

1. __[a]__ lieutenant
2. __[an]__ eclipse
3. __[an]__ albatross
4. __[a]__ chauffeur
5. __[a]__ hexagon

6. __[an]__ application
7. __[a]__ dinosaur
8. __[a]__ musician
9. __[an]__ orphan
10. __[a]__ rainbow

11. __[an]__ elephant
12. __[a]__ folktale
13. __[an]__ egg
14. __[an]__ accident
15. __[a]__ cellular phone

B. Complete each sentence with definite or indefinite articles as indicated.

1. __[The]__ *(definite)* South Pacific has many islands.

2. It is __[a]__ *(indefinite)* part of __[the]__ *(definite)*
   world that has more water than land.

3. Volcanoes and atolls formed __[the]__ *(definite)*
   islands of the South Pacific.

4. __[The]__ *(definite)* animals of __[the]__ *(definite)*
   islands include bats and lizards.

5. Sometimes __[a]__ *(indefinite)* typhoon strikes
   __[the]__ *(definite)* islands.

6. __[An]__ *(indefinite)* atoll is __[a]__ *(indefinite)* coral reef
   that surrounds __[a]__ *(indefinite)* body of water.

7. __[The]__ *(definite)* Great Barrier Reef, __[a]__ *(indefinite)* wall of coral, is in Australia.

8. On __[a]__ *(indefinite)* reef there is __[an]__ *(indefinite)* abundance of wildlife.

9. You might see __[a]__ *(indefinite)* shark hiding in __[the]__ *(definite)* shadows.

10. Would you like to visit __[an]__ *(indefinite)* island in __[the]__ *(definite)* South Pacific?

40. Numerical Adjectives

A **numerical adjective** indicates an exact number. It may refer to the number of persons or things, or it may refer to an arrangement of things in numerical order. Numerical adjectives may be written as numerals or as words.

Gutenberg was the <u>first</u> person to use moveable type to print a book.

About <u>51</u> copies of the Bible he printed are known to exist today.

Underline each numerical adjective.
Circle the noun it modifies.

1. Johann Gutenberg lived in Germany during the <u>fifteenth</u> (century.)

2. At that time books were copied by hand, and it sometimes took a scribe <u>two</u> (years) or more to copy a book.

3. Gutenberg, a skilled inventor and metal worker, spent <u>twenty</u> (years) on his printing experiments.

4. He used small pieces of metal, each with <u>one</u> (letter) on it.

5. His set of type had <u>290</u> different (characters:) letters, punctuation marks, and joined letters required by medieval Latin.

6. He created pages with the type and then printed <u>one</u> (page) at a time on a printing press made from an old wine press.

7. Soon after Gutenberg perfected his press, he had a disagreement with a partner and paid him <u>2,025</u> (guilders,) a great deal of money at that time.

8. Gutenberg printed <u>two</u> (books,) a Bible and another religious work.

9. This Bible had <u>forty-two</u> (lines) of type on each page.

10. Each page had about <u>2,500</u> (characters.)

11. <u>Six</u> (typesetters) worked at the same time to set the type for the Bible.

12. It was printed in <u>three</u> (volumes.)

13. About <u>200</u> (copies) of the Bible may have been printed.

14. Gutenberg's system of typesetting was so good that it was used without significant change until the <u>twentieth</u> (century.)

15. His method of printing survived for more than <u>400</u> (years!)

Johann Gutenberg worked patiently for twenty years on his printing experiments. Give an example of a situation in which you needed patience to achieve your goal.

41. Adjectives as Subject Complements

> An adjective that follows a linking verb and completes the meaning of a sentence is called a **subject complement**. It describes or explains the subject.
>
> SUBJECT (NOUN)   SUBJECT COMPLEMENT (ADJECTIVE)
> **Switzerland   is   mountainous.**

Underline each subject complement. Circle the noun it describes.

1. (Switzerland) is small.

2. The (country) is multilingual: people speak German, French, and Italian.

3. (Switzerland) has been neutral during wars.

4. The country's (government) is democratic.

5. (Switzerland) is wealthy.

6. The (people) are industrious and hardworking.

7. Swiss (banks) have long been famous around the world.

8. Industrial (production) is high.

9. Swiss (products) are excellent.

10. Swiss (chocolate) is delicious.

11. Swiss (watches) are famous.

12. The (watches) are extremely accurate.

13. Many Swiss (watches) are also expensive.

14. Swiss (watchmakers) have always been careful and precise in their work.

15. The (weather) is often rainy.

16. (Winters) are cold and snowy.

17. The (weather) can be foggy in the winter.

18. In winter, skiing (conditions) are excellent.

19. During winter months (resorts) are busy with skiers.

20. The Swiss (countryside) is beautiful.

42. Position of Adjectives

An adjective can be used before a noun or following a linking verb as a subject complement.

Tidal waves are dangerous.

A. Identify the position of each *italicized* adjective. Above the adjective write **BN** if it comes before the noun and **SC** if it is a subject complement.

1. In summer the climate of Florida is *hot*. [SC]

2. The weather is often *humid* too. [SC]

3. During these *hot* [BN] months the beaches are *crowded*. [SC]

4. In winter, temperatures remain *warm*. [SC]

5. Winter nights are usually *cool*. [SC]

6. Florida has thousands of miles of *sandy* [BN] beaches.

7. The *beautiful* [BN] beaches and *warm* [BN] climate attract tourists to Florida.

8. Tourism is *important* [SC] to Florida's economy.

9. Florida has *fabulous* [BN] restaurants with *excellent* [BN] seafood.

10. Vacations in Florida can be *wonderful*. [SC]

B. Underline each adjective that comes before a noun. Circle each adjective that follows a linking verb.

1. The United States is (rich) in natural resources.

2. Large rivers are (useful) for shipping.

3. Northern forests are (valuable) for wood.

4. Coal is a valuable resource that can't be (renewed).

5. Fossil fuels will not be (plentiful) forever.

6. Fertile soils are (rich) in minerals.

7. Certain metals are (vital) to the economy.

8. American mines are (large) and (productive).

9. Natural resources are (important) to everyone.

10. People should be (careful) to use them wisely.

43. Comparative and Superlative Adjectives

Most adjectives have three degrees of comparison: positive, comparative, and superlative. The **positive degree** describes a quality or a characteristic of a noun. The **comparative degree** is used to compare two items or two sets of items. It is formed by adding *-er* after the adjective or *more* or *less* before the adjective. The **superlative degree** is used to compare three or more items. It is formed by adding *-est* after the adjective or *most* or *least* before the adjective.

POSITIVE   **Hydroelectric power, produced by flowing water, isn't very old.**

COMPARATIVE   **The steam engine is older than hydroelectric power.**

SUPERLATIVE   **Power from wind and water are among the oldest types of power.**

A. Write the comparative and superlative degrees of each adjective.

1. sharp _____[sharper]_____ _____[sharpest]_____

2. heavy _____[heavier]_____ _____[heaviest]_____

3. large _____[larger]_____ _____[largest]_____

4. good _____[better]_____ _____[best]_____

5. cold _____[colder]_____ _____[coldest]_____

6. expensive _____[more/less expensive]_____ _____[most/least expensive]_____

7. honest _____[more/less honest]_____ _____[most/least honest]_____

8. peaceful _____[more/less peaceful]_____ _____[most/least peaceful]_____

9. annoying _____[more/less annoying]_____ _____[most/least annoying]_____

10. dangerous _____[more/less dangerous]_____ _____[most/least dangerous]_____

B. On the line write **C** if the *italicized* adjective is in the comparative degree or **S** if it is in the superlative degree.

___[S]___ 1. Water is one of our *most important* natural resources.

___[C]___ 2. The hydroelectric-power process is *cleaner* than the coal-burning process.

___[S]___ 3. Water pollution is one of the country's *biggest* problems.

___[S]___ 4. Thirty years ago Lake Erie was one of the *most polluted* lakes in the country.

___[C]___ 5. Today the water in Lake Erie is much *purer.*

44. More Comparative and Superlative Adjectives

> The comparative degree is used when two persons, places, or things are compared.
>
> **Hurricanes are <u>stronger</u> than tornadoes. They are <u>more destructive</u> too.**
>
> The superlative degree is used when more than two are compared.
>
> **What was the <u>strongest</u> hurricane in history? Was it <u>most destructive</u>?**

Adjectives

A. Circle the correct adjective form in each sentence.

1. Hurricanes are among the (dangerous (most dangerous)) types of storms.

2. Hurricane Katrina, in 2005, was a ((terrible) more terrible) hurricane; it caused more than $100 billion in damage.

3. In some ways, however, it wasn't the (worse (worst)) hurricane in history.

4. Which hurricane was the ((most destructive) more destructive) in history?

5. A 1900 hurricane was ((deadlier) deadliest) than Katrina.

6. That hurricane in Galveston, Texas, resulted in the (higher (highest)) death toll from a hurricane in the United States; about 8,000 people died.

7. No storm has been ((worse) worst) in terms of loss of life.

8. After the storm the city of Galveston built a ((large) largest) seawall.

9. The seawall is the (more elevated (most elevated)) point of land on the island where Galveston is located.

10. The city is ((safer) safest) from violent storms because of the seawall.

B. Complete each sentence with the correct form of the adjective.

1. The sinking of the *Titanic* was one of the _____[most shocking]_____ (shocking) events in the 20th century.

2. It was also _____[worse]_____ (bad) than any other tragedy at sea; more than 1,500 people died.

3. When the *Titanic* was built in 1912, it was the _____[biggest]_____ (big) passenger ship in the world.

4. It was also one of the _____[most luxurious]_____ (luxurious) ships.

5. Nowadays ships are _____[safer]_____ (safe) than the *Titanic* because they carry enough lifeboats for everyone aboard.

45. Little, Less, Least and Few, Fewer, Fewest

> **Count nouns** name things that can be counted. They have plural forms. Use *few, fewer, fewest* to compare count nouns. **Noncount nouns** name things that cannot be counted. They do not have plural forms. Use *little, less, least* to compare noncount nouns.
>
> Tom has a few quarters.   Tom has very little change.
> Tom has fewer quarters than   Tom has less change than Joe does.
> Joe does.
> Tom has the fewest quarters   Tom has the least change of all
> of all the boys.   the boys.

A. Write *little* or *few* to complete each sentence.

1. Deserts get very _____[little]_____ rain.

2. Only a _____[few]_____ animals can live in a desert environment.

3. _____[Little]_____ vegetation grows in the desert.

4. _____[Few]_____ types of plants can survive the harsh conditions.

5. Many desert plants have very _____[few]_____ leaves.

B. Write *less* or *fewer* to complete each sentence.

1. The carpenter had _____[fewer]_____ hammers than screwdrivers.

2. He had _____[fewer]_____ tools than the other workers had.

3. He made _____[less]_____ progress than the others made.

4. He also gave the others _____[less]_____ advice.

5. I think he made _____[less]_____ money than anyone else.

C. Write *least* or *fewest* to complete each sentence.

1. My aunt has the _____[least]_____ jewelry of the three women.

2. She owns the _____[fewest]_____ rings of all.

3. She also has the _____[fewest]_____ bracelets.

4. She puts the _____[least]_____ importance on material things.

5. She has the _____[fewest]_____ needs of anyone I know.

Adjectives

46. Demonstrative Adjectives

> A **demonstrative adjective** points out the thing it refers to.
> The demonstrative adjectives are *this*, *that*, *these* and *those*.
> *This* and *that* point out one person, place, or thing.
> *These* and *those* point out more than one person, place, or thing.
> *This* and *these* name persons, places, or things that are near.
> *That* and *those* name persons, places, or things that are far.
>
> **This rock is a special kind of rock—a fossil.**
> **That rock contains a rare mineral, gold.**
> **These rocks are made of quartz.**
> **Those rocks are nothing but gravel.**

Adjectives

A. Underline each demonstrative adjective.

1. That scientist is a geologist.

2. The formation of this planet is a geologist's field of study.

3. These scientists collect rock samples for study.

4. Fossilized plants and animals help these people reconstruct the past.

5. Fossils are important in this kind of work.

6. Dating those specimens provides useful information to scientists.

7. Many areas of science benefit from this knowledge.

8. That insect was preserved in fossilized tree sap.

9. The name of that fossil is amber.

10. Those plants and animals preserved as fossils lived millions of years ago.

B. Complete each sentence with a demonstrative adjective.

1. _____[That]_____ *(far)* scientist is a mineralogist.

2. _____[This]_____ *(near)* branch of geology is the study of minerals.

3. _____[Those]_____ *(far)* crystals are formed from minerals.

4. _____[This]_____ *(near)* pencil contains a mineral—graphite.

5. _____[These]_____ *(near)* rocks contain iron, another important mineral.

47. Those and Them

> *Those* is used to point out something. *Those* may be an adjective or a pronoun. *Them* is always a pronoun. The personal pronoun *them* can never be used as an adjective.
>
> ADJECTIVE NOUN MODIFIED   PRONOUN
> **Those** **jackets are on sale.** **Those by the escalators are on sale too.**
>
> PERSONAL PRONOUN USED AS AN OBJECT
> **I have two new jackets. I bought them at the sale.**

A. Circle the correct word in each sentence.

1. (Those) Them) flowers bloom in the fall.

2. Do you know (those) them) people?

3. Did you see (those) them) boys playing soccer?

4. I have known (those (them)) for years.

5. Who wrote (those) them) adventure stories?

6. Cory saw (those (them)) on television.

7. I have some of (those) them) kinds of stamps in my collection.

8. Jane walked with (those (them)) through the park.

9. The principal congratulated (those (them)) for their good grades.

10. (Those) Them) sentences were not difficult.

B. Complete each sentence with *those* or *them*.

1. ____[Those]____ kinds of athletic shoes are expensive.

2. We sent an invitation to ____[them]____.

3. Do you prefer these or ____[those]____?

4. Are you going to continue fixing ____[those]____ two cars?

5. The answers are missing. Can you supply ____[them]____?

6. He walked by his friends without noticing ____[them]____.

7. Are ____[those]____ CDs for sale?

8. My father talked to ____[them]____ about moving to Texas.

9. I am not sure if Mom will like these or ____[those]____.

10. Deciding between ____[them]____ will be difficult.

Adjectives

48. Interrogative Adjectives

> An **interrogative adjective** is used in asking a question. The interrogative adjectives are *which, what,* and *whose. Which* is used in asking about one or more of a specific set of persons or things. *What* is used in asking about people or things that are not necessarily limited to a specific set or group. *Whose* refers to possession.

Adjectives

A. Underline each interrogative adjective. Circle the noun it modifies.

1. Which (state) in the United States is the largest?

2. In which (state) was the first U.S. president inaugurated?

3. What (animal) is on the California state flag?

4. Whose (home) in Virginia is named Monticello?

5. Which (group) of islands forms a state?

6. Which (state) is called the Cradle of Presidents because so many presidents have come from there?

7. Whose (residence) is located in Washington, D.C.?

8. What (city) is the capital of Texas?

9. In which (city) is the Alamo located?

10. In what (state) was the Declaration of Independence approved?

B. Complete each sentence with an interrogative adjective. For some sentences, more than one answer may be correct.

1. _____[Which/What]_____ state has Raleigh as its capital?

2. In _____[which/what]_____ state is the Sears Tower located?

3. _____[Which/What]_____ land did Thomas Jefferson purchase for the United States?

4. In _____[what]_____ year did Texas become a state?

5. In _____[whose]_____ honor was Washington, D.C., named?

6. In _____[which/what]_____ state will you find the Empire State Building?

7. _____[Whose]_____ portrait is on a dime?

8. In _____[what]_____ year did World War II end?

9. _____[Which/What]_____ state is the smallest?

10. _____[Which/What]_____ state do you live in?

49. Indefinite Adjectives

> **Indefinite adjectives** refer to all or any of a group of persons, places, or things. Some of the most common indefinite adjectives are *all, another, any, both, each, either, every, few, many, most, neither, no, other, several,* and *some.*

Read each proverb. Circle each indefinite adjective and underline the noun that it goes with. One proverb has more than one indefinite adjective.

1. Time cures (all) <u>things</u>.

2. The rain falls on (every) <u>roof</u>.

3. A rolling stone gathers (no) <u>moss</u>.

4. One person's trash is (another) <u>person's</u> treasure.

5. (Many) <u>hands</u> make light work.

6. (Every) <u>bird</u> likes to hear itself sing.

7. Turn the (other) <u>cheek</u>.

8. Only a fool tests the depth of the water with (both) <u>feet</u>.

9. (No) <u>news</u> is good news.

10. (Each) <u>day</u> provides its own gifts.

11. There are (many) <u>paths</u> to the top of the mountain, but the view is the same.

12. (Some) <u>things</u> are better left unsaid.

13. (Any) <u>plan</u> is bad that cannot be changed.

14. We have (other) <u>fish</u> to fry.

15. (All) <u>work</u> and (no) <u>play</u> make Jack a dull boy.

16. (Every) <u>dog</u> has its day.

17. Tomorrow is (another) <u>day</u>.

18. (All) good <u>things</u> must come to an end.

19. You can't have it (both) <u>ways</u>.

20. There is (no) <u>proverb</u> without a grain of truth.

Adjectives

50. Adjective Phrases

> A prepositional phrase is made up of a preposition, its object, and any modifiers of the object. An **adjective phrase** is a prepositional phrase that describes a noun or a pronoun.
>
> **Ancient Rome was a busy city <u>with many large buildings</u>.**

Underline the adjective phrase in each sentence. Circle the noun it goes with.

1. Rich Romans had large, brick (houses) <u>with red tile roofs</u>.

2. (Paintings) <u>of flowers</u> often decorated the walls.

3. (Mosaics) <u>in bright colors</u> covered the floors.

4. Several (generations) <u>of one family</u> often lived together.

5. A poor family most likely had an (apartment) <u>of only one room</u>.

6. Such families used (water) <u>from public fountains</u>.

7. The (shops) <u>in the neighborhood</u> provided carryout food.

8. The (Forum) <u>at Rome's center</u> was the main meeting place.

9. It was a (place) <u>for public speaking</u>.

10 The (job) <u>of the speakers</u> was to convince the audience.

11. One (goal) <u>of a Roman boy's education</u> was to become a good speaker.

12. Daily (life) <u>in the country</u> had a slower pace than city life had.

13. Slaves usually ran the (farms) <u>of the rich</u>.

14. Families visited their farms to enjoy (rest) <u>from the city's bustle</u>.

15. Children's toys included board games, kites, and tiny (models) <u>of people and animals</u>.

16. Boys played various (games) <u>with balls</u>.

17. Girls had (dolls) <u>of wax or clay</u>.

18. Romans enjoyed many (kinds) <u>of entertainment</u>.

19. Most events were free, so (people) <u>with little money</u> could attend them.

20. The Circus Maximus, a (racecourse) <u>in Rome</u>, could seat some 250,000 people.

51. Reviewing Adjectives

A. On the line describe the *italicized* adjective as descriptive, numerical, indefinite, demonstrative, or interrogative.

_____[numerical]_____ 1. E. L. Konigsburg wrote the book *From the Mixed-up Files of Mrs. Basil E. Frankweiler* about *two* children who run away from home.

_____[interrogative]_____ 2. In *which* museum does the story take place?

_____[demonstrative]_____ 3. *That* museum is the Metropolitan Museum of Art in New York City.

_____[descriptive]_____ 4. The children, Claudia and Jamie, have a *wonderful* adventure.

_____[indefinite]_____ 5. They spend *several* days roaming the hallways of the museum.

_____[descriptive]_____ 6. The children see a *beautiful* sculpture of an angel.

_____[demonstrative]_____ 7. They want to find out about *that* sculpture.

_____[descriptive]_____ 8. Is it by the *Italian* artist Michelangelo?

_____[descriptive]_____ 9. Are they *clever* enough to solve the mystery?

_____[interrogative]_____ 10. *What* secret lies behind the sculpture?

B. Above each *italicized* adjective write **BN** if the adjective is before a noun or **SC** if it is a subject complement.

11. The room in the museum was *[SC]* *enormous.*

12. An *[BN]* *unusual* object attracted our attention.

13. The object was *[SC]* *Egyptian.*

14. It was like a *[BN]* *small* dollhouse with statues of people inside.

15. The object was for the use of the *[BN]* *dead* person in the afterlife.

C. Underline each indefinite adjective. Circle the noun or nouns it refers to.

16. Many (paintings) at our art center depict pastoral scenes.

17. There are only a few (images) of city streets with tall buildings.

18. Among the modern paintings are those of several local (artists.)

19. Besides the oils and watercolors, our tiny museum tries to display at least one other (form) of art.

20. I like both (forms,) oils and watercolors, but I'm also interested in other types of art.

CONTINUED

D. Complete each sentence with *this, that, these,* or *those.*

21. _____[This]_____ *(near)* room contains arms and armor.

22. _____[That]_____ *(far)* chain mail armor differs from
_____[this]_____ *(near)* plate armor.

23. _____[These]_____ *(near)* helmets all have visors, but
_____[those]_____ *(far)* helmets do not.

24. Look! _____[That]_____ *(far)* horse is wearing special armor.

25. Even _____[these]_____ *(near)* shoes are made of metal.

E. Complete each sentence with the correct degree of comparison.

26. What is the _____[most/least popular]_____ *(popular)* exhibit in the museum?

27. The Egyptian statues are _____[older]_____ *(old)* than
the Greek statues.

28. Susi thought that the vases were the _____[prettiest]_____ *(pretty)* objects
in the entire blown-glass display.

29. For Rob the Egyptian room was the _____[best]_____ *(good)*
part of the museum.

30. For me the armor was _____[more/less interesting]_____ *(interesting)*
than the sculpture.

Try It Yourself

Write three sentences about a museum, a park, or another place you visited recently.
Describe it. Tell what you found most interesting, most exciting, and so on.
Be sure to use adjectives correctly.

_____

_____

_____

Check Your Own Work

Choose a selection from your writing portfolio, your journal, a work in progress,
an assignment from another subject, or a letter. Revise it, applying the skills you
have reviewed. This checklist will help you.

✔ Have you chosen vivid descriptive adjectives?

✔ Have you been careful to use the correct article?

✔ Have you used correct forms for possessive and demonstrative adjectives?

✔ Have you chosen the correct degree of comparison for adjectives?

52. Principal Parts of Verbs; Verb Phrases

> A **verb** shows action or state of being. The principal parts of a verb are the **present**, the **present participle**, the **past**, and the **past participle**. The present participle is formed by adding *-ing* to the base form. The past and the past participle of **regular verbs** are formed by adding *-d* or *-ed* to the base form.
>
> | PRESENT | PRESENT PARTICIPLE | PAST | PAST PARTICIPLE |
> |---------|-------------------|------|-----------------|
> | jump | jumping | jumped | jumped |
> | cry | crying | cried | cried |
> | hum | humming | hummed | hummed |
>
> A **verb phrase** is two or more verbs used together as a unit. A verb phrase may have one or more **auxiliary**, or **helping**, **verbs** and a main verb. The present participle is often used with auxiliary verbs such as forms of *be.* The past participle is often used with auxiliary verbs such as forms of *has.* Other common auxiliary verbs are *can, could, may, might, should, will,* and the forms of *do.*
>
> We usually <u>wait</u> for my dad here. (present)
> We <u>waited</u> here yesterday. (past)
> We <u>are waiting</u> for him now. (form of *be* and the present participle)
> We <u>have waited</u> for an hour. (form of *have* and the past participle)

Underline the verb or verb phrase in each sentence. Identify the main verb as present, present participle, past, or past participle.

_____[past]_____ 1. On April 18, 1906, San Francisco <u>experienced</u> a terrible earthquake.

_____[past]_____ 2. Around 5 a.m. a foreshock <u>occurred</u>.

___[present participle]___ 3. Within a few seconds the ground <u>was quaking</u> violently.

___[past participle]___ 4. In less than a minute thousands of buildings <u>had toppled</u>.

_____[past]_____ 5. Water mains and gas lines <u>shattered</u>.

___[present participle]___ 6. Soon a huge fire <u>was raging</u>.

___[past participle]___ 7. By April 21 the fire <u>had destroyed</u> more than 500 city <u>blocks</u>.

_____[past]_____ 8. About 6,000 people <u>died</u> in the tragedy.

_____[present]_____ 9. Scientists today <u>warn</u> us about fault lines, probable earthquake sites.

_____[present]_____ 10. Another such earthquake <u>remains</u> possible.

53. More Verb Phrases

A verb phrase contains the main verb and an auxiliary, or helping, verb. Following are common auxiliary verbs.

be	are	has	do	will	can	shall	may
am	was	have	did	would	could	should	might
is	were	had					must
	been						

A. Underline each verb phrase.

1. Chimney sweeps <u>have cleaned</u> chimneys for hundreds of years.

2. People <u>should clean</u> their chimneys periodically.

3. Burning wood in a fireplace <u>can leave</u> soot on the chimney walls.

4. After a few years this soot <u>can ignite</u>.

5. A serious fire <u>could be</u> the result.

6. Homeowners <u>must hire</u> a chimney sweep.

7. The number of chimneys <u>has declined</u>.

8. Likewise, the number of chimney cleaners <u>has decreased</u>.

9. Many cities <u>have passed</u> strict laws regarding wood-burning stoves and fireplaces.

10. Traditionally chimney sweeps <u>would be</u> children.

11. They <u>would go</u> into the chimney.

12. Nowadays chimney sweeps <u>are using</u> sophisticated equipment, including video cameras, in their jobs.

13. Chimney cleaners <u>should</u> not <u>be</u> afraid of heights.

14. They often <u>must work</u> on steep roofs.

15. The demand for chimney sweeps usually <u>will be</u> greatest before the start of winter.

B. Circle the auxiliary verb in each sentence.

1. Nursing (can) be a rewarding profession.

2. Nurses (must) study for at least two years, and some study for four years.

3. Nurses (might) work with people of all ages—from babies to the elderly.

4. In the past, nursing (had) been a profession for women.

5. Now many men as well as women (are) entering the profession.

Name _____

54. Regular and Irregular Verbs

The past and the past participle of regular verbs are formed by adding *-d* or *-ed* to the present. There is no general rule for forming the past and the past participle of **irregular verbs.** Check a dictionary if you are not sure of these forms.

	PRESENT	PAST	PRESENT PARTICIPLE	PAST PARTICIPLE
REGULAR	**walk**	**walked**	**walking**	**walked**
IRREGULAR	**ride**	**rode**	**riding**	**ridden**

A. Write the present participle, the past, and the past participle of each verb.

	PRESENT	PRESENT PARTICIPLE	PAST	PAST PARTICIPLE
1.	drift	[drifting]	[drifted]	[drifted]
2.	ring	[ringing]	[rang]	[rung]
3.	rise	[rising]	[rose]	[risen]
4.	stop	[stopping]	[stopped]	[stopped]
5.	choose	[choosing]	[chose]	[chosen]
6.	talk	[talking]	[talked]	[talked]
7.	write	[writing]	[wrote]	[written]
8.	make	[making]	[made]	[made]
9.	go	[going]	[went]	[gone]
10.	fly	[flying]	[flew]	[flown]

B. Complete each sentence with the present participle, the past, or the past participle of the verb shown in parentheses.

1. The Old North Church has _____[stood]_____ (stand) in Boston for hundreds of years.

2. One cold night before the American Revolution, Paul Revere was _____[waiting]_____ (wait) for a signal.

3. Someone _____[put]_____ (put) lanterns in the steeple to signal the arrival of British troops.

4. Revere _____[rode]_____ (ride) off to warn the people of the British invasion of Massachusetts.

5. According to tradition, he was _____[shouting]_____ (shout) "The British are coming! The British are coming!" as he rode through towns.

55. Lie, Lay and Sit, Set

The verb *lie (lying, lay, lain)* means "to rest or recline." It doesn't have an object.

Please lie on the floor for the warm-up exercise.

The verb *lay (laying, laid, laid)* means "to put in place or position." It takes a direct object.

He laid the books on the table and sat down to study.

The verb *sit (sitting, sat, sat)* means "to have or keep a seat."

Please sit here and have some cookies and milk.

The verb *set (setting, set, set)* means "to put or place in position."

I set the timer for five minutes.

A. Complete each sentence with the correct form of *lie* or *lay*.

1. Matt, please _____[lay]_____ the newspaper on the table.

2. The tourists have _____[lain]_____ on the beach all afternoon.

3. Most of Europe _____[lies]_____ in the north temperate zone.

4. I _____[laid]_____ my glasses somewhere, but I don't remember where.

5. If you are really so sick, I think that you should _____[lie]_____ in bed.

6. Mrs. Greene _____[laid]_____ out the bride's wedding dress and then helped her get ready.

7. Jeff, where did you _____[lay]_____ my coat?

8. My father _____[lay]_____ on the couch to watch TV, but he fell asleep.

9. To relax, you should _____[lie]_____ quietly, close your eyes, and meditate for a few minutes.

10. The cook _____[laid]_____ out a lunch of sandwiches and salads.

B. Complete each sentence with the correct form of *sit* or *set*.

1. Please _____[set]_____ the buckets in the broom closet.

2. I _____[sit]_____ in the front row so that I can take pictures.

3. We _____[sat]_____ on the 50-yard line at the football game last Sunday!

4. I _____[set]_____ the two flower pots on either side of the front door.

5. Please _____[set]_____ that box on the table and help me move this bed.

56. Rise, Raise; Let, Leave; and Teach, Learn

The verb *rise (rising, rose, risen)* means "to ascend or move up."
This road rises very steeply, so cars cannot travel fast.

The verb *raise (raising, raised, raised)* means "to lift up, put up, or elevate."
Please raise your hand if you want to participate.

The verb *let (letting, let, let)* means "to permit or allow."
My dad let me stay up late to watch the movie.

The verb *leave (leaving, left, left)* means "to depart from or to allow to be."
The train left the station on time.

The verb *teach (teaching, taught, taught)* means "to give instruction."
Carla taught her little brother to play catch.

The verb *learn (learning, learned, learned)* means "to receive instruction or to gain knowledge."
He learned to swim when he was 10 years old.

A. Circle the correct verb in parentheses.

1. (Rise (Raise)) the flag quickly and lower it slowly.

2. ((Let) Leave) me try that trick.

3. Maureen ((left) let) for school without her lunch.

4. Please ((rise) raise) and say the Pledge of Allegiance.

5. My dad ((taught) learned) me to ride a bicycle.

B. Complete the sentence with the correct verb in the past tense.

1. Slowly the Loch Ness monster _____[rose]_____ from the murky depths.

2. The ship _____[left]_____ the harbor, on its way to England.

3. My brother _____[taught]_____ me how to play air hockey.

4. The temperature _____[rose]_____ 12 degrees this morning.

5. I _____[left]_____ school early today to keep a dental appointment.

6. The bridge keeper _____[raised]_____ the bridge so the boat could sail by.

7. We _____[left]_____ early for the game because traffic was heavy.

8. After I _____[learned]_____ to play chess, I joined the chess club.

9. The speaker _____[rose]_____ from her chair to begin the main address.

10. Dad _____[let]_____ me set up the tent.

57. Transitive Verbs

> A **transitive verb** expresses an action that passes from a doer to a receiver. Every transitive verb has a receiver of its action. The receiver is the direct object.
>
> | DOER | TRANSITIVE VERB | RECEIVER (DIRECT OBJECT) |
> |------|-----------------|--------------------------|
> | **Eli Whitney** | **invented** | **the cotton gin.** |

A. Underline the transitive verb in each sentence. Write **D** above the doer and **R** above the receiver of the action.

1. Eli Whitney [D] earned a college degree [R] in 1792.
2. He [D] learned the newest ideas [R] in science and technology.
3. But he [D] needed a job [R].
4. Phineas Miller [D] helped him [R].
5. Miller [D] managed a large plantation [R] in Georgia.
6. Whitney [D] studied the operation [R] of the plantation.
7. English companies [D] wanted American cotton [R].
8. These companies [D], however, did not want the seeds [R] in the cotton.
9. Whitney [D] got an idea [R] for a machine.
10. His machine [D] removed all the seeds [R] quickly and easily.
11. Eli Whitney's work [D] helped the English companies [R].
12. Cotton planters [D] grew more and more cotton [R].
13. Cotton planters [D] did not pay Whitney [R] for his machines.
14. They [D] simply copied the design [R] of his machine.
15. Later, some states [D] paid him for his invention.

B. Choose the best verb to complete each sentence. Write it in the past tense. Use each verb once. Underline the direct object of each verb.

fit   invent   make   need   put

1. In 1797 the U.S. government ___[needed]___ guns for its army.

2. At that time a worker made each part of a gun individually and ___[put]___ the parts together.

3. Eli Whitney ___[invented]___ a system that used machines.

4. Each machine ___[made]___ only one part.

5. The parts ___[fit]___ any gun.

58. Intransitive Verbs

An **intransitive verb** has no receiver of its action. It does not have a direct object. An intransitive verb may be followed by an adverb or a prepositional phrase.

Laura Ingalls Wilder wrote about the American Midwest.

A. Underline the intransitive verb in each sentence.

1. Young Laura Ingalls lived in the Midwest in the late 1800s.

2. Her family farmed.

3. The family's house sat in the woods.

4. Later the family moved from the woods to the prairies farther west.

5. As a young woman, Laura married.

6. Later she wrote about pioneer life.

7. She drew on her experiences as a girl.

8. Her descriptions of the joys and hardships of pioneer life appeal to readers.

9. For example, *Little House on the Prairie* tells about her trip west from Wisconsin in a covered wagon.

10. Laura Ingalls Wilder died in 1957.

B. Underline the intransitive verb(s) in each sentence.

1. The Amazon River starts in the Peruvian Andes.

2. From the Andes it flows east.

3. It travels across northern Brazil.

4. Finally, after almost 4,000 miles, it arrives at the Atlantic Ocean.

5. The river widens and deepens considerably.

6. In fact, large freighters sail in its waters.

7. The Amazon goes through lush rain forests.

8. Thousands of different creatures live in the Amazon.

9. Catfish, electric eels, and piranhas swim in its waters.

10. Millions of unique plants grow in the rain forest along its shore.

59. Verbs That Can Be Transitive or Intransitive

Some verbs can be transitive or intransitive, according to their use in a sentence.

TRANSITIVE **Madge ate the cookies.** (*Ate* is transitive because it has a direct object, *cookies*, which is the receiver of the action.)

INTRANSITIVE **We ate at seven o'clock last night.** (*Ate* is intransitive; it does not have a direct object, a receiver of the action.)

A. Underline the verb in each sentence. On the line write **T** if it is transitive or **I** if it is intransitive.

__[I]__ 1. In spring, wildflowers <u>grow</u> along this highway.

__[T]__ 2. We <u>grow</u> flowers in our garden.

__[T]__ 3. The parents <u>hid</u> the presents from their children.

__[I]__ 4. Some animals <u>hide</u> from their predators by means of their color.

__[I]__ 5. Our class <u>sings</u> every morning.

__[T]__ 6. The class <u>sang</u> the national anthem yesterday.

__[T]__ 7. Jana <u>wrote</u> me an e-mail.

__[I]__ 8. Jana always <u>writes</u> on the computer.

__[T]__ 9. Picasso <u>painted</u> priceless masterpieces.

__[I]__ 10. Picasso <u>painted</u> in a variety of styles.

B. Underline the verb in each sentence. On the line write **T** if it is transitive or **I** if it is intransitive. For transitive verbs, circle the receiver (the direct object).

__[T]__ 1. Florence Nightingale, a British woman, <u>founded</u> modern nursing (methods) in the 1800s.

__[I]__ 2. She <u>rebelled</u> against the idle life of her wealthy family.

__[T]__ 3. Nightingale <u>dedicated</u> her (life) to the service of others.

__[I]__ 4. With 38 nurses she <u>traveled</u> to Turkey during a war there.

__[T]__ 5. They <u>nursed</u> wounded (soldiers.)

__[T]__ 6. At first, doctors didn't <u>accept</u> Nightingale's (nurses.)

__[I]__ 7. Nightingale's work <u>resulted</u> in improvements in hospitals.

__[I]__ 8. The death rate for ill soldiers <u>fell</u> by two thirds.

__[T]__ 9. She <u>raised</u> (funds) for supplies for soldiers.

__[T]__ 10. She <u>won</u> the (respect) of the British public for her work.

Verbs

60. Linking Verbs

A linking verb links the subject of a sentence with a subject complement (a noun, a pronoun, or an adjective). The most common linking verbs are forms of *be* (*am*, *is*, *are*, *was*, and *were*).

SUBJECT	LINKING VERB	SUBJECT COMPLEMENT
John F. Kennedy	**was**	the 35th **president** of the United States.

The following verbs can also be used as linking verbs: *appear, become, continue, feel, grow, look, remain, seem, smell, sound,* and *taste.*

SUBJECT	LINKING verb	SUBJECT COMPLEMENT
He	**became**	**president** in 1961.

Circle each linking verb. Above each *italicized* subject complement write its part of speech: **N** for noun, **P** for pronoun, or **A** for adjective.

1. John F. Kennedy (was) [N] *president* from 1961 to 1963.

2. He (became) an [N] *officer* in the navy during World War II.

3. He (was) extremely [A] *brave* during the war.

4. After the war he (became) a [N] *politician.*

5. He (became) a U.S. [N] *representative* at the age of 29.

6. Kennedy (was) the country's [N] *president* at 44 years of age.

7. He (is) [A] *famous* for his inspiring speeches.

8. The founder of the Peace Corps (was) [P] *he.*

9. Though a war injury caused terrible back pain, he always (looked) [A] *energetic.*

10. He (remained) an [N] *advocate* for civil rights for all Americans.

11. He also (became) an avid [N] *promoter* of space exploration.

12. The leader who set the goal of landing astronauts on the moon (was) [P] *he.*

13. He (was) the [N] *author* of two best-selling books.

14. He (remained) [N] *president* until his assassination in 1963 in Dallas.

15. Americans (felt) very [A] *sad* about his death.

John F. Kennedy succeeded despite a serious limitation—severe back pain from a war injury. Everyone has limitations of one sort or another. Give an example of a limitation you have and what you can do to overcome it.

Name _____

61. Reviewing Transitive, Intransitive, and Linking Verbs

A. Underline the verb in each sentence. On the line write **T** if it is transitive, **I** if it is intransitive, or **L** if it is linking.

___[T]___ 1. People throughout much of the world eat salmon.

___[T]___ 2. Fishers catch millions of salmon each year.

___[L]___ 3. Salmon fishing remains an important industry.

___[I]___ 4. Many salmon live in the north part of the Pacific Ocean.

___[L]___ 5. The Atlantic salmon are native to the North Atlantic Ocean.

___[L]___ 6. Chinook are the largest species of salmon.

___[T]___ 7. Salmon lay their eggs in fresh water.

___[I]___ 8. The eggs hatch in fresh water.

___[I]___ 9. Some salmon travel up rivers during mating season.

___[L]___ 10. Salmon fishing is a popular sport on the Pacific coast.

B. Five of these sentences contain linking verbs.
Underline each linking verb and circle its complement.

11. The salmon is (famous) for its long and difficult journeys.

12. At spawning time salmon swim upstream.

13. They can leap over 10-foot waterfalls.

14. The male salmon is the (protector) of the female during spawning.

15. She deposits her eggs in a stream bed.

16. The male then fertilizes the eggs.

17. The eggs hatch after three or four months.

18. The young salmon are (food) for many predators.

19. The young salmon travel to the ocean and grow (large.)

20. Species of salmon sometimes become (rare) because of overfishing.

Name _____

62. Simple Tenses

The **simple present tense** tells about an action that happens again and again and about things that are general truths.
    Russia now <u>elects</u> its leader.

The **simple past tense** tells about an action that happened in the past.
    Czars <u>ruled</u> imperial Russia.

The **simple future tense** tells about an action that will happen in the future.
    Continuing reforms <u>will help</u> Russia to a better government.

Verbs

A. Underline the verb in each sentence. Write the tense on the line.

[simple past]   1. Czars <u>had</u> power in Russia until 1917.

[simple past]   2. In 1917, revolutionaries <u>overthrew</u> the czar.

[simple past]   3. Communists <u>became</u> dominant in the new government.

[simple past]   4. Communists <u>controlled</u> Russia for more than 70 years.

[simple past]   5. In 1991 the Soviet Union <u>ended</u>.

[simple past]   6. Russia <u>became</u> a republic.

[simple present]   7. The Communist party no longer <u>rules</u> in Russia.

[simple present]   8. The Russian people <u>want</u> a democratic government.

[simple future]   9. <u>Will</u> the Russians <u>build</u> a democratic system?

[simple future]   10. The answer <u>will appear</u> in the years to come.

B. Complete each sentence with the tense of the verb indicated.

control   1. OPEC, the Organization of Petroleum Exporting Countries, _____[controls]_____ the oil production of many nations. *(present)*

join   2. Many oil-producing countries _____[joined]_____ OPEC. *(past)*

meet   3. Representatives from each of the member countries _____[meet]_____ from time to time to discuss oil production. *(present)*

discuss   4. They _____[discuss]_____ the levels of oil production. *(present)*

decide   5. Sometimes they _____[decide]_____ to lower production. *(present)*

make   6. Such a decision _____[will make]_____ oil prices increase. *(future)*

cut   7. In the 1970s OPEC _____[cut]_____ production. *(past)*

go   8. As a result, gas prices in the United States _____[went]_____ up. *(past)*

be   9. There _____[were]_____ long lines of cars at the gas pumps. *(past)*

reduce   10. _____[Will]_____ new car designs _____[reduce]_____ the need for gasoline? *(future)*

Name _____

63. Progressive Tenses

The **progressive tenses** are formed with the present participle and a form of *be*. The **present progressive tense** tells about something that is happening right now. It uses the present tense of *be (am, is, are)* and the present participle.

> **The children are reciting nursery rhymes.**

The **past progressive tense** tells about something that was happening in the past. It uses the past tense of *be (was, were)* and the present participle.

> **They were sitting in a circle at the start of the program.**

The **future progressive tense** tells about something that will be happening in the future. It uses *will be, is going to be,* or *are going to be* with the present participle.

> **The teacher will be asking several students to perform.**
> **Are the children going to be illustrating their favorite rhymes?**

A. Underline each verb in the progressive tense. On the line tell if the verb is in the present progressive tense, the past progressive tense, or the future progressive tense.

____[present]____ 1. Mrs. Johnson is reading nursery rhymes to the children in preschool.

____[future]____ 2. She will be displaying posters that go with what she reads.

____[present]____ 3. The children are enjoying the rhymes.

____[past]____ 4. When I was growing up, I liked to listen to nursery rhymes too.

____[past]____ 5. While the teacher was reading, I recited the words with her.

B. Complete each sentence with the correct progressive tense of the verb at the left.

go 1. Jack and Jill _____[were going]_____ up the hill with an empty pail. *(past)*

grow 2. Mary, Mary, Quite Contrary _____[is growing]_____ silver bells in her garden. *(present)*

sit 3. While Humpty Dumpty _____[was sitting]_____ on a wall, he had a great fall. *(past)*

try 4. All the king's horses and all the king's men _____[are trying]_____ to put him together again. *(present)*

eat 5. Little Miss Muffett _____[was eating]_____ curds and whey while she sat on a tuffet. *(past)*

fall 6. According to the old rhyme, London Bridge _____[is falling]_____ down. *(present)*

laugh 7. The little boy _____[will be laughing]_____ as the cow jumps over the moon. *(future)*

sit 8. Little Jack Horner _____[was sitting]_____ in a corner as he ate a pie. *(past)*

get 9. Mother Hubbard _____[will be getting]_____ her dog a bone. *(future)*

fly 10. Look! Four and twenty blackbirds _____[are flying]_____ out of the pie! *(present)*

Name _____

64. Perfect Tenses

The **perfect tenses** are formed with the past participle and a form of *have.* The **present perfect tense** tells about an action that happened at some indefinite time in the past or an action that started in the past and continues into the present time. It uses the present tense of *have (has, have)* and the past participle.

Marge has made a delicious chocolate cake.

The **past perfect tense** tells about a past action that was completed before another past action started. It uses the past tense of *have (had)* and the past participle.

Homer had eaten three slices before we even got one.

A. Underline each verb in the perfect tense. On the line tell whether the verb is in the present perfect tense or the past perfect tense.

_____[present]_____ 1. My mother's family has had a family reunion for many years.

_____[past]_____ 2. My mother's great-grandfather had started the tradition long before I was born.

_____[present]_____ 3. My family has gone to the reunion for many years.

_____[present]_____ 4. We have had a lot of fun every time we attended!

_____[present]_____ 5. The reunions have been at the local picnic grounds for the last five years.

_____[present]_____ 6. Cousin Ona has won the sack race many times, but I am determined to win the next race.

_____[past]_____ 7. Earlier this year no one had remembered that the picnic grounds needed to be reserved.

_____[past]_____ 8. By the time we arrived, other people had taken our usual spot.

_____[past]_____ 9. After everyone from our family had arrived, we decided to hold the picnic in our backyard.

_____[past]_____ 10. Aunt Joan had prepared seven quarts of potato salad because she expected a huge crowd.

B. Complete each sentence with the correct perfect tense of the verb at the left.

ask 1. Many eager fans ____[have asked]____ the famous movie star for her autograph. *(present)*

try 2. She ____[has tried]____ to avoid them. *(present)*

avoid 3. She ____[has avoided]____ leaving her hotel room. *(present)*

gather 4. Anxiously, the fans ____[had gathered]____ outside her hotel as afternoon approached. *(past)*

hope 5. They ____[had hoped]____ to get her autograph before she left for the Academy Awards ceremony. *(past)*

Name _____

65. More Perfect Tenses

Complete each sentence with the indicated tense.

sing   1. Our school's chorus _____[has sung]_____ on TV. (present perfect)

sing   2. It _____[had sung]_____ the same song in a concert held last month. (past perfect)

choose 3. We _____[have chosen]_____ the date for the picnic. (present perfect)

choose 4. We _____[had chosen]_____ the same picnic grove we used two years ago. (past perfect)

damage 5. Floods _____[had damaged]_____ the town before this year's record flood nearly submerged it. (past perfect)

damage 6. This year's flood _____[has damaged]_____ the entire downtown area. (present perfect)

finish 7. I ____[have]____ not ____[finished]____ all my homework yet. (present perfect)

finish 8. I _____[had finished]_____ my science project before I started my math assignment. (past perfect)

ride   9. I ____[have]____ never ____[ridden]____ the new roller coaster at Adventure Park. (present perfect)

ride   10. Once, after I _____[had ridden]_____ a roller coaster three times in a row, I got sick. (past perfect)

eat   11. Allison ____[had]____ not ____[eaten]____ sushi before she tasted it last week. (past perfect)

eat   12. She _____[has eaten]_____ sushi twice since then! She really likes it! (present perfect)

take   13. My brother _____[has taken]_____ a few piano lessons, and he can play several songs. (present perfect)

take   14. He ____[had]____ never ____[taken]____ a music lesson before he attended the concert. (past perfect)

travel 15. My friends _____[have traveled]_____ in a helicopter several times. (present perfect)

travel 16. They ____[had]____ not ____[traveled]____ in one until they received free tickets. (past perfect)

see   17. I ____[had]____ never ____[seen]____ a live shark before I went to the aquarium yesterday. (past perfect)

see   18. Now I _____[have seen]_____ both very large and very small sharks. (present perfect)

break   19. The students _____[have broken]_____ three beakers in the lab. (present perfect)

break   20. Before they dropped the beakers today, they ____[had]____ never _____[broken]_____ a single one. (past perfect)

66. Reviewing Tenses

Complete each sentence with the tense of the verb indicated in parentheses.

interest   1. The planet Mars _____ [has interested] _____ humans for thousands of years. (present perfect)

be   2. Mars _____ [is] _____ Earth's neighbor and the seventh-largest planet in the solar system. (simple present)

find   3. In the 1800s people thought that scientists _____ [had found] _____ canals on Mars and that this discovery provided proof of life there. (past perfect)

see   4. What the scientists _____ [had seen] _____ were channels, not dug-out canals. (past perfect)

write   5. Long before humans launched spacecraft, science fiction writers _____ [were writing] _____ about life on Mars. (past progressive)

write   6. H. G. Wells _____ [wrote] _____ *The War of the Worlds,* a book about an invasion of Earth by creatures from Mars. (simple past)

invade   7. In Ray Bradbury's stories *The Martian Chronicles,* inhabitants from Earth _____ [were invading] _____ Mars. (past progressive)

send   8. Since the 1960s several countries _____ [have sent] _____ spacecraft to explore Mars. (present perfect)

pass   9. In 1965 the U.S. spacecraft *Mariner 4* _____ [passed] _____ within 9,920 kilometers of the planet's surface. (simple past)

take   10. It _____ [took] _____ 22 close-up photos that showed a cratered surface. (simple past)

conduct   11. Landers from the United States, *Viking 1* and *Viking 2,* _____ [conducted] _____ experiments on Mars soil during the 1970s. (simple past)

conduct   12. Currently the United States _____ [is conducting] _____ a series of probes of Mars with the *Odyssey* spacecraft. (present progressive)

continue   13. The spacecraft, which reached Mars in 2001, _____ [will continue] _____ to provide valuable information about the planet. (future)

wonder   14. People still _____ [are wondering] _____ about the possibility of life on Mars. (present progressive)

find   15. _____ [Will] _____ these spacecraft _____ [find] _____ any life there? (future)

Verbs

67. Subject-Verb Agreement

A verb agrees with its subject in person and number. The base form of a verb is used for the present tense with both singular and plural subjects. The present tense verb for a third person singular subject, however, is formed by adding -s or -es to the base form of the verb.

THIRD PERSON SINGULAR	A senator <u>serves</u> for six years.
THIRD PERSON PLURAL	Two senators from each state <u>serve</u> in Congress.

Verbs

A. Underline the verb in each sentence. In the first column write **S** if the subject is singular or **P** if it is plural. In the second column identify the person of the subject: **1** for first person, **2** for second person, and **3** for third person.

	NUMBER	PERSON
1. We <u>study</u> U.S. government in school.	[P]	[1]
2. The president <u>serves</u> for four years.	[S]	[3]
3. Citizens <u>elect</u> representatives for two-year terms.	[P]	[3]
4. The representatives <u>have</u> the possibility of reelection.	[P]	[3]
5. Supreme Court justices <u>get</u> lifetime appointments.	[P]	[3]
6. The Senate <u>confirms</u> the justices.	[S]	[3]
7. Some politicians <u>stay</u> in office for many years.	[P]	[3]
8. Strom Thurmond of South Carolina <u>was</u> a member of Congress for nearly 50 years.	[S]	[3]
9. <u>Are</u> you <u>surprised</u> by that fact?	[S/P]	[2]
10. He <u>was</u> in the U.S. Senate from 1954 to 2003.	[S]	[3]

B. If the underlined noun is singular, make it plural. If it is plural, make it singular. Change the verb to agree with the new subject. Write your answers on the lines.

	NEW SUBJECT	NEW VERB
1. A <u>president</u> takes on many responsibilities.	[presidents]	[take]
2. The <u>presidents</u> hold the executive power.	[president]	[holds]
3. A <u>senator</u> meets with voters.	[senators]	[meet]
4. <u>Members</u> of the House meet with voters.	[member]	[meets]
5. A <u>citizen</u> needs to express opinions.	[citizens]	[need]

Name _____

68. More Subject-Verb Agreement

A subject and its verb must always agree in person and number. When a sentence starts with *there* and a form of the verb *be (is, are, was, were),* the subject follows the verb. The form of *be* must agree with the subject.

There was an English colony in Massachusetts in the 1600s.
There were several children on board the *Mayflower*.

A. Underline the subject in each sentence. Circle the correct verb in parentheses.

1. Among the early settlers (was (were)) Pilgrims from England.

2. Plymouth ((was) were) the site of the first permanent settlement of Europeans in New England.

3. Nowadays this old town ((is) are) a tourist attraction.

4. Many visitors ((come) comes) to see the town.

5. These tourists ((see) sees) Plymouth Plantation, a reconstruction of the original settlement.

6. The old houses (is (are)) also popular attractions.

7. This historic place ((has) have) more than a tourist-based economy, however.

8. Boatyards ((line) lines) the shore.

9. Fishing ((was) were) important during much of Plymouth's past.

10. Many fishing boats ((continue) continues) to dock in Plymouth Harbor.

B. Circle the correct verb in parentheses.

1. There (was (were)) more than 100 Pilgrims on the *Mayflower*.

2. The Pilgrims arrived in Plymouth in December. There (was (were)) many problems for them at first.

3. There ((was) were) no place to live. They had to clear the land and build a fort.

4. There ((was) were) very little food that winter.

5. There ((is) are) a replica of the *Mayflower* in Plymouth Harbor today.

6. There (is (are)) many things to see and do in Plymouth.

7. There (is (are)) many restored colonial houses.

8. There ((is) are) also a large state forest nearby.

9. There ((is) are) a monument to the Pilgrims in the center of Plymouth.

10. There (is (are)) several museums, including a wax museum.

69. Doesn't and Don't; You as the Subject

Verbs

If the subject is in the third person singular, use *doesn't*. For all other third person singular and plural subjects, use *don't*.

THIRD PERSON SINGULAR **Alice doesn't get up early.**
OTHER SINGULAR AND PLURAL **I don't have an alarm clock**
You don't have to wake me, however.
The children don't get up early.

Use *are* and *were* with the subject *you*, whether *you* is singular or plural.

SINGULAR **You are always late, Jennifer.**
PLURAL **You are late again, Jennifer and Carla.**

A. Complete each sentence with *doesn't* or *don't*.

1. A pine tree _____[doesn't]_____ shed its needles in winter.

2. A pine tree's needles _____[don't]_____ get brown either.

3. An evergreen tree _____[doesn't]_____ lose its color in winter.

4. During winter most other trees in northern
   climates _____[don't]_____ keep their leaves.

5. When a tree loses its leaves in fall, it _____[doesn't]_____ die.

6. The tree _____[doesn't]_____ produce new leaves until spring.

7. All trees will die, however, if they _____[don't]_____ get water.

8. If rain _____[doesn't]_____ provide enough moisture, even a pine tree may turn brown.

9. During a drought, trees will die if people _____[don't]_____ water them.

10. We _____[don't]_____ need to water the tree in our yard this summer
    because we have had plenty of rain.

B. Circle the correct verb in parentheses.

1. (Is (Are)) you going on a field trip today with your class?

2. You (is (are)) the best speller in class.

3. Sally and Nancy, (is (are)) you going to wear your jackets?

4. Jim, (was (were)) you in the library this afternoon?

5. ((Were) Was) you at the game yesterday?

70. Agreement with Compound Subjects Connected by *And*

> Compound subjects connected by the word *and* usually require a verb that agrees with a plural subject.
>
> **England and France** <u>were</u> allies in World War I.

A. Circle the correct verb in parentheses.

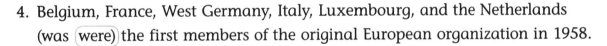

1. Germany and Austria-Hungary (was (were)) allies in World War I.

2. Germany and France (was (were)) enemies in World Wars I and II.

3. World War I and World War II (was (were)) so terrible that the countries of Europe realized they needed to work together.

4. Belgium, France, West Germany, Italy, Luxembourg, and the Netherlands (was (were)) the first members of the original European organization in 1958.

5. England and Spain (was (were)) admitted later.

6. England, France, Germany, and Italy now ((work) works) together in the European Union.

7. Austria, Germany, England, and France (is (are)) no longer enemies.

8. Political cooperation and economic unity ((represent) represents) basic goals of the European Union.

9. People and goods ((move) moves) freely among the countries in the Union.

10. As a result, war and conflict (has (have)) become less likely in Europe.

B. Circle the correct verb. Add words to complete the sentences. [Answers will vary.]

1. World War I and World War II (was (were)) _____.

2. England, France, and Germany (has (have)) _____.

3. The European Union and the United States (is (are)) _____.

4. Belgium and Luxembourg (has (have)) _____.

5. France and Germany ((share) shares) _____.

Verbs

71. Agreement with Indefinite Pronouns

> The indefinite pronouns *each, either, neither, anyone, no one, anybody, nobody, everyone, everybody, someone,* and *somebody* are always singular. They require verbs that agree with singular subjects.
>
> **Each of the students has a responsibility in the classroom.**
> **Someone unlocks the school doors at 8.**
> **Nearly everyone arrives by 8:45.**

A. Complete each sentence with the correct present tense form of the verb at the left.

know 1. Everyone _____[knows]_____ our school's routine.

say 2. Everybody _____[says]_____ the Pledge of Allegiance in the morning.

raise 3. Someone _____[raises]_____ the flag before classes start.

sing 4. Everyone _____[sings]_____ the national anthem before a major sports event.

take 5. Each of the teachers _____[takes]_____ attendance.

lower 6. At the end of the day someone _____[lowers]_____ the flag.

follow 7. Each of the classes _____[follows]_____ an end-of-the-day routine too.

erase 8. Somebody _____[erases]_____ the boards daily.

go 9. Almost everyone _____[goes]_____ home at 3:30.

leave 10. The principal and the assistant principal stay later; neither of them _____[leaves]_____ until five o'clock.

B. Write about the routine at your school. Circle the correct verb. Add words to complete the sentences. [Answers will vary.]

1. Almost everybody (arrives) arrive) _____.

2. Hardly anybody (come (comes)) _____.

3. Somebody (clean (cleans)) _____.

4. Everyone (is) are) _____.

5. Everybody (sing (sings)) _____.

72. Agreement with Special Nouns

> Nouns such as *deer, fish, sheep, trout, salmon, cod, moose, corps,* and certain proper nouns such as *Portuguese, Chinese, Swiss,* and *Iroquois* have the same form in the singular and the plural. The sense of the sentence indicates whether the subject is singular or plural.

A. Underline the subject in each sentence. Write **S** above the subject if it is singular and **P** if it is plural. Circle the correct verb in parentheses.

1. A famous <u>Sioux</u> [S] (was) were) Crazy Horse, who led his tribe in a war against the U.S. government.

2. Red <u>salmon</u> [P] (is (are) caught in Puget Sound.

3. The <u>Iroquois</u> [P] (was (were) allies of the British in the wars of the 1700s.

4. Look! A <u>deer</u> [S] (is) are) eating grass in the backyard.

5. The <u>Spanish</u> [P] (lives (live) on the Iberian Peninsula.

6. The <u>Sioux</u> [P] ((belong) belongs) to the group called the Plains Indians.

7. <u>Trout</u> [P] ((live) lives) mainly in fresh water.

8. A <u>moose</u> [S] ((is) are) a member of the deer family.

9. <u>Reindeer</u> [P] (was (were) brought from Siberia to Alaska.

10. Some <u>sheep</u> [P] (is (are) waiting to be sheared.

11. <u>Deer</u> [P] (is (are) timid by nature.

12. These <u>fish</u> [P] (is (are) such a lovely orange-red color.

13. A <u>Portuguese</u>, [S] Bartolomeu Dias, ((is) are) remembered for his explorations.

14. The <u>Chinese</u> [P] ((inhabit) inhabits) the world's most populous country.

15. A small <u>goldfish</u> [S] ((was) were) raised by the class in this fish tank.

B. Circle the correct verb. Add words to complete the sentence. [Answers will vary.]

1. This deer (live (lives)) _____.

2. A Sioux ((is) are) _____.

3. The Chinese ((live) lives) _____.

4. That small sheep ((has) have) _____.

5. Trout ((swim) swims) _____.

Verbs

75

73. Reviewing Subject-Verb Agreement

A. Circle the correct verb in parentheses.

1. African Americans ((celebrate) celebrates) a holiday in December.

2. ((Are) Is) you familiar with the holiday?

3. Its name ((is) are) Kwanzaa.

4. There (is (are)) seven days of celebration.

5. Each of the days ((is) are) devoted to a different principle, such as unity, creativity, or faith.

6. On December 31 everybody ((participates) participate) in a feast.

7. There (is (are)) special plays and speeches at the feast.

8. Children (doesn't (don't)) receive gifts until January 1.

9. The Swahili ((celebrate) celebrates) a similar harvest holiday, as do other African peoples.

10. The feast ((doesn't) don't) have a long history in this country; it began in 1966.

B. Complete each sentence with the correct present tense form of the verb at the left.

house   11. This building ____[houses]____ stray dogs and cats.

want   12. Each of the children ____[wants]____ to use the computer.

be   13. There ____[are]____ 10 tomatoes on the counter.

be   14. ____[Are]____ you ready for the class play?

be   15. The flowers and the vase ____[are]____ on the coffee table.

be   16. Everyone ____[is]____ going to get an ice-cream sundae.

have   17. The French ____[have]____ many great paintings in their museums.

be   18. Look! There ____[is]____ a shooting star!

need   19. This fish ____[needs]____ some food in its tank.

crow   20. A rooster ____[crows]____ every morning.

74. Active and Passive Voice

> **Voice** shows whether the subject of a sentence is the doer or the receiver of the action expressed by the verb. When a verb is in the **active voice**, the subject is the doer of the action. When a verb is in the **passive voice**, the subject is the receiver of the action.
>
> ACTIVE VOICE   **Ancient Rome had many public baths.**
> PASSIVE VOICE   **The baths were visited by both men and women.**

A. Each sentence is written in the passive voice. Rewrite it in the active voice.

1. Admission was charged by the owner of the bath.

   [The owner of the bath charged admission.]

2. Steam rooms and saunas were provided by some baths.

   [Some baths provided steam rooms and saunas.]

3. Hair-cutting salons were featured at other baths.

   [Other baths featured hair-cutting salons.]

4. A variety of goods was sold by shopkeepers.

   [Shopkeepers sold a variety of goods.]

5. The baths were used by most Romans every day.

   [Most Romans used the baths every day.]

B. Each sentence is written in the active voice. Rewrite it in the passive voice.

1. Shops lined the streets of Rome.

   [The streets of Rome were lined with shops.]

2. Men wore cotton or wool tunics.

   [Cotton or wool tunics were worn by men.]

3. Slaves taught children reading, writing, and arithmetic.

   [Children were taught reading, writing, and arithmetic by slaves.]

4. They used pebbles to do math problems.

   [Pebbles were used to do math problems.]

5. Their mothers taught girls to spin and weave.

   [Girls were taught to spin and weave by their mothers.]

Verbs

75. Indicative Mood

> **Mood** shows the manner in which an action or a state of being is expressed. The **indicative mood** of a verb is used when the speaker is making a statement or asking a question. Most sentences are in the indicative mood. Verbs in the indicative mood can be in any tense, and they can be active or passive.
>
> **What are the big cats of Africa?** (question, simple present tense)
> **She read about lions, leopards, and cheetahs.** (statement, simple past tense, active)
> **These cats have been hunted for their skins.** (statement, present perfect tense, passive)

Underline the verb in the indicative mood in each sentence. Write the tense on the line. Add the correct end punctuation.

[simple present]   1. Do you know about the small cats of Africa?

[present perfect]   2. I have learned about several kinds.

[simple present]   3. The African wild cat has the largest territorial range.

[simple past]   4. African wild cats were the ancestors of domestic cats.

[present progressive]   5. We are checking the map for locations of the African golden cat.

[past perfect]   6. I had never heard of servals before.

[simple present]   7. Where do they live?

[present perfect]   8. They have been seen throughout Sub-Saharan Africa.

[simple past]   9. One observer watched a serval near a pond.

[past perfect]   10. By the end of three hours, the cat had eaten 28 frogs.

[simple present]   11. Caracals are the largest of the small cats.

[simple present]   12. How much do they weigh?

[present perfect]   13. They have been known to weigh 40 pounds.

[simple present]   14. Caracals are famous for catching low-flying birds.

[past perfect]   15. Had you heard of any other small African cats?

[past progressive]   16. Earlier I was reading about sand cats.

[simple present]   17. These cats are found in the deserts of North Africa.

[present perfect]   18. How have they adapted to the severe desert climate?

[simple present]   19. Thick hair protects the bottom of their feet.

[simple present]   20. Sand cats go without water for long periods of time.

Verbs

76. Emphatic Form of the Indicative Mood

The **emphatic form** of the indicative mood gives special force to a simple present or past tense verb. To make an emphatic form in the present tense, use *do* or *does* before the base form of the verb in a statement. To make an emphatic form in the past tense, use *did* before the base form of the verb.

Many people do want to know more about Antarctica.
The United States did establish a research station there in the 1950s.

A. Underline the verb phrase in the emphatic form in each sentence. On the line write whether the verb phrase is in the present tense or the past tense.

___[present]___ 1. Antarctica does have the coldest weather on earth.

___[past]___ 2. Once the temperature did drop to –126.9° Fahrenheit.

___[present]___ 3. Summer temperatures do average around freezing.

___[present]___ 4. The cold does make it almost impossible for humans to live there.

___[present]___ 5. Several species of penguins and seals do spend part of the year in Antarctica.

___[past]___ 6. The ancient Greeks did think there was land to the far south.

___[past]___ 7. In 1773 Captain James Cook did sail around the continent, but he could not land because of the ice.

___[present]___ 8. Historians do believe that Captain John Davis landed on Antarctica in 1821.

___[past]___ 9. In 1911 explorers did reach the South Pole.

___[present]___ 10. Scientists today do study Antarctica's climate and geology.

B. Rewrite each sentence. Change the *italicized* verb to the emphatic form.

1. Two kinds of fish *thrive* in the cold waters around Antarctica.

   [Two kinds of fish do thrive in the cold waters around Antarctica.]

2. Fishing fleets *wanted* to know more about these fish.

   [Fishing fleets did want to know more about these fish.]

3. Scientists *equipped* seals with video cameras.

   [Scientists did equip seals with video cameras.]

4. These "seal cams" *helped* the scientists learn about the fish.

   [These "seal cams" did help the scientists learn about the fish.]

5. Some animals *have* unusual jobs!

   [Some animals do have unusual jobs!]

Verbs

Name _____

77. Imperative Mood

The **imperative mood** is used to express a command or a request. To form the imperative mood, use the base form of a verb. The subject of an imperative sentence is understood to be the second person pronoun, *you.*

Tell me how to find the North Star.　　**Locate the Big Dipper.**
Please focus the telescope.　　　　　**Find a protractor.**

A command can be given in the first person by using *let's (let us)* before the base form of a verb.

Let's buy a star chart.

Rewrite each sentence in the imperative mood. [**Answers may vary.**]

1. You can find out your latitude.

   [Find out your latitude.]
   _____

2. First you should tie a 15-inch piece of string to the middle of the flat side of a protractor.

   [Tie a 15-inch piece of string to the middle of the flat side of a protractor.]
   _____

3. Then you need to tie an eraser or other small weight to the loose end of the string.

   [Tie an eraser or other small weight to the loose end of the string.]
   _____

4. You should then hold the straight edge of the protractor near your eye.

   [Hold the straight edge of the protractor near your eye.]
   _____

5. You must be sure that the curved side is down.

   [Be sure that the curved side is down.]
   _____

6. You have to point the protractor directly at the North Star.

   [Point the protractor directly at the North Star.]
   _____

7. Next you need to pinch the string against the side of the protractor to mark the angle.

   [Pinch the string against the side of the
   _____

   protractor to mark the angle.]
   _____

8. You should then read the angle on the protractor.

   [Read the angle on the protractor.]
   _____

9. You have to use the number that is less than 90°.

   [Use the number that is less than 90°.]
   _____

10. Finally you need to subtract that number from 90° to find your latitude.

    [Subtract that number from 90° to find your latitude.]
    _____

Verbs

78. Subjunctive Mood

> The **subjunctive mood** is used in several ways: (1) to express a wish or desire;
> (2) to express a request, a command, or a suggestion after the word *that;*
> or (3) to express something that is contrary to fact (not true). The subjunctive
> refers to something that is hoped or wished rather than what actually is.
>
> For the verb *be,* the common forms of the subjunctive are *be* and *were. Be* is used
> with verbs of command, request, or suggestion. Otherwise, *were* is used. In many
> sentences with *if* clauses, the auxiliary verb *would* is used in the second clause.
>
> **I wish I were able to play the piano better.** (a wish)
> **My mom suggested that I be more willing to practice.**
> (a suggestion after *that*)
> **If I were a concert pianist, I would make her proud.**
> (something contrary to fact)

A. Underline the subjunctive verb or verb phrase in each sentence. Write **W** for a
wish or desire; **R** for a request, command, or suggestion after *that;* or **C** for something
contrary to fact.

___[W]___ 1. I wish my dog were better behaved.

___[C]___ 2. If she were better behaved, I would enter her in the dog show.

___[R]___ 3. My mother suggested I be more diligent about training her.

___[C]___ 4. If she were still a puppy, I would take her to obedience school.

___[C]___ 5. If I were more patient, I'd work with her every day.

___[R]___ 6. My dad insists that she be kept off the furniture.

___[W]___ 7. He wishes she were kept in the kitchen at all times.

___[C]___ 8. If she were smaller, the problem would not be as bad.

___[R]___ 9. I begged that he be more tolerant with her.

___[W]___ 10. I wish we were all in agreement on this matter.

B. Underline the correct form of the verb for the subjunctive and then complete
each sentence with your own idea. [**Sample answers are given.**]

1. If I (was were) President of the United States, I would
   _____ [fly on *Air Force One* as often as possible] _____.

2. I wish my school (was were) _____ [closer to my house] _____.

3. I recommend that top athletes (be are) _____ [excellent students as well] _____.

4. I wish my class (was were) _____ [going to Washington, D.C., on a field trip] _____.

5. If I (was were) a better singer, I'd _____ [join the school choir] _____.

79. Modal Auxiliaries

> **Modal auxiliaries** are used to express possibility, permission, ability, necessity, obligation, intention, and willingness. They are followed by main verbs in the base form. Common modal auxiliaries are *may, might, can, could, must, should, will,* and *would.*
>
> POSSIBILITY We **might** watch a movie tonight.
> PERMISSION Mom says we **may** make some popcorn.
> ABILITY We **can** pop it right in the bag in the microwave.
> NECESSITY We **must** leave the kitchen as neat as we found it.
> OBLIGATION We **should** clean the inside of the microwave.
> INTENTION I **will** wash the bowls and glasses.
> WILLINGNESS **Would** you please help me with the beverages?

A. Underline the modal auxiliary in each sentence once. Underline the main verb twice. On the line write what the verb phrase expresses—possibility, permission, ability, necessity, obligation, intention, or willingness.

_____[necessity]_____ 1. We must prepare for our yard sale tomorrow.

_____[obligation]_____ 2. We should sort all the things into categories.

_____[intention]_____ 3. I will separate the books into fiction and nonfiction.

_____[willingness]_____ 4. Would you arrange the CDs and DVDs?

_____[permission]_____ 5. Dad said we may sell this old lawn mower.

B. Complete each sentence with a modal auxiliary, according to the meaning given in parentheses. More than one modal auxiliary may be correct for some sentences.

1. _____[Would]_____ you like a job as a babysitter? *(willingness)*

2. Every babysitter _____[should]_____ take a first-aid class. *(obligation)*

3. A babysitter _____[must]_____ watch the children at all times. *(necessity)*

4. Some parents _____[may]_____ allow you to take the children outdoors. *(possibility)*

5. Others _____[might]_____ tell you to stay in the house. *(possibility)*

6. A babysitter _____[must]_____ follow the parent's instructions. *(necessity)*

7. What _____[will]_____ you do to entertain the children? *(intention)*

8. You _____[could]_____ plan some activities for them. *(possibility)*

9. You _____[can]_____ amuse children with some simple items. *(ability)*

10. You _____[might]_____ want to take a game you can play with them. *(possibility)*

Verbs

Name _____

80. Reviewing Verbs

A. Underline the verb or verb phrase in each sentence. If there is an auxiliary verb, write it on the line.

_____ 1. Michelangelo <u>lived</u> in Italy.

[can] 2. You <u>can see</u> one of his famous works, the *Pietà*, in Rome.

[will] 3. You <u>will feel</u> amazement at the sculpture's power.

[has] 4. The sculpture <u>has traveled</u> to the United States.

[could] 5. People <u>could see</u> it in New York at a World's Fair in the 1960s.

B. Write the forms for each verb.

	PRESENT PARTICIPLE	PAST	PAST PARTICIPLE
6. sing	[singing]	[sang]	[sung]
7. walk	[walking]	[walked]	[walked]
8. grow	[growing]	[grew]	[grown]
9. drop	[dropping]	[dropped]	[dropped]
10. put	[putting]	[put]	[put]

C. Underline the verb in each sentence. On the line write **T** if the verb is transitive or **I** if it is intransitive.

_[T]_ 11. Michelangelo <u>carved</u> magnificent statues.

_[I]_ 12. He also <u>painted</u>.

_[T]_ 13. He <u>painted</u> the ceiling of the Sistine Chapel in Rome.

_[T]_ 14. Michelangelo <u>depicted</u> the story of creation and other Bible stories on the ceiling of the chapel.

_[I]_ 15. He <u>died</u> in 1564.

D. Read each sentence. On the line write **IN** for indicative, **IM** for imperative, or **SU** for subjunctive.

_[IN]_ 16. Have you seen any of Michelangelo's works?

_[IN]_ 17. His statue of David is in Florence, Italy.

_[IM]_ 18. Look at a picture of it on the Internet.

_[SU]_ 19. I wish I were in Italy.

_[SU]_ 20. If I were in Italy, I would go to Florence.

Verbs

E. On the line identify the tense of the *italicized* verb in each sentence— simple present, simple past, future, present progressive, past progressive, present perfect, or past perfect.

_____[present perfect]_____ 21. People *have known* about peanuts since ancient times.

_____[simple present]_____ 22. A peanut *is* not actually a nut.

_____[simple present]_____ 23. Peanuts *belong* to the legume—bean—family.

_____[past progressive]_____ 24. Peanuts *were growing* in the Americas long before the Europeans settled here.

_____[past perfect]_____ 25. They *had grown* in South America before they were introduced to North America.

_____[simple past]_____ 26. In the United States, peanuts first *grew* in the South.

_____[simple past]_____ 27. George Washington Carver *created* more than 300 products from peanuts— including printer's ink and soap.

_____[present perfect]_____ 28. People *have eaten* peanuts as snacks since the 1860s.

_____[present perfect]_____ 29. Peanut butter *has teamed* with jelly in sandwiches since the 1920s.

_____[future]_____ 30. People *will enjoy* peanut products for years to come.

Try It Yourself

Write three sentences about a painting or a sculpture you like. Describe the work of art. Tell why you like it. Be sure to use verbs correctly.

_____

_____

_____

Check Your Own Work

Choose a selection from your writing portfolio, your journal, a work in progress, an assignment from another subject, or a letter. Revise it, applying the skills you have reviewed. This checklist will help you.

✔ Have you used correct forms of the irregular and regular verbs?

✔ Have you been careful when you used any of the troublesome verbs?

✔ Have you correctly formed verbs in the different tenses?

✔ Do all of your subjects and verbs agree in number?

Verbs

81. Adverbs of Time

> An **adverb** is a word that describes, or modifies, a verb, an adjective, or another adverb. **Adverbs of time** answer the question when or how often. They usually modify verbs.
>
> **She has already read a few books of myths.** (modifies *has read*)
> **She often reads Aesop's fables.** (modifies *reads*)
>
> Adverbs of time include *again, already, always, before, early, ever, finally, first, frequently, immediately, later, never, now, once, recently, seldom, sometimes, soon, still, today,* and *usually.*

A. Circle the adverb of time in each sentence. Underline the verb it modifies.

1. People have (always) been curious about the natural world.

2. Ancient myths—or stories—(often) attempted to explain things in nature.

3. Ancient people, including the Greeks, (frequently) created stories about the origins of the world and the things in it.

4. (Later) the ancient Romans borrowed myths from the Greeks.

5. The main characters of these myths were (usually) gods or heroes.

6. Have you (ever) seen a horse with wings?

7. Well, the mythical horse Pegasus (sometimes) flew through the air.

8. The names of the planets (still) reflect the influence of mythology.

9. (First,) the telling of myths was part of an oral tradition.

10. (Finally,) poets such as Homer recorded the myths.

B. Circle the correct adverb of time.

1. We have ((already) ever) begun our study of classical art.

2. Many classical sculptures are ((now) early) in the British Museum.

3. The sculpture of ancient Greece has ((seldom) yesterday) been equaled.

4. Visitors to Greece can see examples of classical statues ((today) ever).

5. ((Once) Always) I saw a picture of the Venus de Milo, an ancient statue of a goddess. Its arms are missing.

6. People ((often) before) wonder what it would have looked like with arms.

7. Another famous statue, the Winged Victory, ((now) never) lacks its head.

8. People ((usually) already) think that classical statues were white.

9. Scholars believe that the ancients ((always) now) painted the statues.

10. When the statues were found, the paint had ((already) never) worn off.

Name _____

82. Adverbs of Place

Adverbs of place answer the question *where*. They usually modify verbs.

> **Please don't play catch <u>inside</u>.** (modifies *play*)
> **You can walk <u>there</u>.** (modifies *can walk*)

Adverbs of place include *above, away, back, below, down, far, forward, here, in, inside, outside, there, up,* and *within*.

A. Circle each adverb of place.
Underline the verb it modifies.

1. The eagle <u>soared</u> (upward) in its flight.

2. The little boy's dog <u>ran</u> (away.)

3. Bright stars <u>twinkled</u> (overhead.)

4. <u>List</u> all your suggestions (below.)

5. Orioles <u>build</u> nests (high) in the trees.

6. Beautiful paper lanterns <u>hung</u> (here) and (there) among the trees.

7. Because of the blizzard we <u>didn't go</u> (outside) for two days.

8. <u>Place</u> the table (here,) please.

9. The boy <u>went</u> (inside) for his boots.

10. Please <u>look</u> (up) when you finish the exercise.

B. Circle the correct adverb of place in each sentence.

1. Our neighbors have just moved ((away) downward).

2. Please look (inside (outside)) and see if it is raining.

3. You've gone the wrong way. You need to walk ((back) here) two blocks.

4. We looked (away (around)) for the missing books.

5. The batter swung too ((low) down) and missed the ball. He was out!

6. The two new polar bears are (upward (there)) on the rocks.

7. The kittens should not be left ((outside) below) in the rain.

8. Please sign your name ((here) forward), Ms. Bergen.

9. Don't look ((down) far) or you'll get dizzy.

10. We were so cold that we had to go ((inside) far).

Adverbs

83. Adverbs of Manner

Adverbs of manner answer the question how or in what manner. They usually modify verbs. Many, but not all, adverbs of manner end in *-ly*. Three common exceptions are *fast*, *well*, and *hard*.

> **She learned math quickly.** (modifies *learned*)
> **She worked hard all afternoon.** (modifies *worked*)

Some adverbs of manner are *anxiously, bravely, cheerfully, correctly, courageously, diligently, fast, gracefully, kindly, steadily, swiftly, truthfully,* and *unexpectedly.*

A. Write an adverb of manner for each adjective.

1. proud _____[proudly]_____
2. excited _____[excitedly]_____
3. happy _____[happily]_____
4. soft _____[softly]_____
5. intelligent _____[intelligently]_____

6. easy _____[easily]_____
7. beautiful _____[beautifully]_____
8. diligent _____[diligently]_____
9. tireless _____[tirelessly]_____
10. thoughtful _____[thoughtfully]_____

B. Circle each adverb of manner. Underline the verb it modifies.

1. Barbara McClintock, a scientist, <u>worked</u> (carefully) and (determinedly.)

2. She (deservedly) <u>won</u> a Nobel Prize for Medicine in 1983 for her work.

3. An intelligent woman, she (quickly) <u>earned</u> a Ph.D.—in two years.

4. Genetics interested her, and she <u>studied</u> cells (intently.)

5. She <u>worked</u> (hard) in her laboratory.

6. She (painstakingly) <u>examined</u> the genetic structure of corn.

7. In 1931 she (brilliantly) <u>explained</u> a genetic process called crossing-over, which was the discovery that earned her the Nobel Prize.

8. Many scientists (foolishly) <u>rejected</u> her ideas.

9. She (patiently) <u>rechecked</u> her research.

10. Later discoveries by other scientists (clearly) <u>supported</u> her work.

Barbara McClintock continued to work even when others said that she was wrong. She showed that she had tremendous confidence in herself. Name one or two ways you can show that you have confidence in yourself.

Adverbs

87

84. Adverbs of Degree

Adverbs of degree answer the question how much or how little.
They may modify verbs, adjectives, or other adverbs.

He was <u>barely</u> moving. (modifies *was moving*, a verb)
The story is <u>rather</u> interesting. (modifies *interesting*, an adjective)
He traveled <u>quite</u> extensively. (modifies *extensively*, an adverb)

Adverbs of degree include *almost, awfully, barely, extraordinarily, extremely, fairly, fully, greatly, hardly, incredibly, merely, much, partly, quite, rather, really, scarcely, somewhat, terribly, too,* and *very.*

Circle each adverb of degree. Underline the word it modifies.
Identify the word that is modified by writing **V** above it if it is a verb,
Adj if it is an adjective, or **Adv** if it is an adverb.

1. Spain is (rather) <u>famous</u> [Adj] for the exploration of North and South America.

2. Spaniards did not discover America; they (merely) <u>explored</u> [V] it.

3. The civilizations in the Americas were (quite) <u>complex</u> [Adj].

4. Some Spanish explorers and writers have left (fairly) <u>concise</u> [Adj] accounts of the civilizations in the Americas.

5. Spain's exploration in other parts of the world is (hardly) <u>discussed</u> [V].

6. Ruy Gonzalez de Clavijo, however, (rather) <u>daringly</u> [Adv] traveled to the Middle East in the 15th century.

7. Gonzalez, a Spanish diplomat, went from Spain to Turkey and Iran in 1403, a time when travel was (awfully) <u>difficult</u> [Adj].

8. He met Tamburlaine, an Islamic king, who was (very) <u>powerful</u> [Adj].

9. Tamburlaine had built an (extremely) <u>large</u> [Adj] empire in Asia.

10. He was a fierce fighter who was (greatly) <u>feared</u> [V] by his enemies.

11. Tamburlaine treated his enemies (terribly) <u>cruelly</u> [Adv].

12. He wanted to make his capital at Samarkand (incredibly) <u>beautiful</u> [Adj].

13. The mosque there has (extraordinarily) <u>lovely</u> [Adj] mosaics of turquoise and gold.

14. Gonzalez wrote a (really) <u>wonderful</u> [Adj] account of his visit to Tamburlaine's kingdom.

15. Many people have never heard about this (quite) <u>unusual</u> [Adj] trip.

85. Adverbs of Affirmation and Negation

Adverbs of affirmation and negation tell whether a statement is true or false. The **adverbs of affirmation** include *allegedly, indeed, positively, undoubtedly,* and *yes.*

    You **undoubtedly** know who Annie Oakley is.

The **adverbs of negation** include *no, not,* and *never.*

    I have **never** heard of her.

A. Underline each adverb of affirmation or negation.
Above each write **A** if it indicates affirmation or **N** if it indicates negation.

    [A]
1. Yes, Annie Oakley was an American sharpshooter and entertainer.

    [A]
2. Indeed, she could shoot dimes tossed into the air.

3. She was a star of Buffalo Bill Cody's Wild West show, and her

             [N]
   sharpshooting feats never failed to amaze audiences.

            [N]
4. Her real name was not Annie Oakley; it was Phoebe Ann Moses.

  [A]
5. Undoubtedly, she was an amazing person.

B. Underline each adverb. Write on the line what it indicates—**T** for time, **P** for place, **M** for manner, **D** for degree, **A** for affirmation, or **N** for negation.

__[D]__ 1. The Northwest Ordinance of 1787 had a very important role in the history of Ohio, Indiana, Illinois, Michigan, and Wisconsin.

__[T]__ 2. First, the Ordinance organized the distribution of land in the territory.

__[P]__ 3. The land there was divided according to a grid system.

__[M]__ 4. Land was carefully divided into townships—squares of six miles on each side.

__[T]__ 5. Next, each township was divided into individual sections—one mile on each side.

__[T]__ 6. One of these sections was always set aside for schools.

__[M]__ 7. People quickly bought the individual sections.

__[M]__ 8. The Ordinance also carefully specified the procedure for new states to join the Union.

__[T]__ 9. Finally, the Ordinance granted key civil rights to the residents of the territory, including freedom of religion.

__[A]__ 10. Indeed, the Northwest Ordinance of 1787 prohibited slavery in the area.

Name _____

86. Comparative and Superlative Adverbs

Some adverbs can be compared. The **comparative degree** compares the quality of two actions or conditions. The **superlative degree** compares three or more. To form the comparative degree or the superlative degree of adverbs that do not end in *-ly,* add *-er* or *-est.* To form the comparative or superlative of adverbs that end in *-ly,* add *more* or *most* (or *less* or *least*) before the adverb.

If I use a computer, I can work <u>faster</u> than I can if I use a typewriter.
A computer can do this work <u>more efficiently</u> than a typewriter can.

Two common adverbs that have irregular comparative and superlative forms are *well* and *badly: well, better, best; badly, worse, worst.*

A. On the lines write the comparative and the superlative forms of each adverb.

COMPARATIVE	SUPERLATIVE
1. early	[earlier]	[earliest]
2. wisely	[more/less wisely]	[most/least wisely]
3. badly	[worse]	[worst]
4. fast	[faster]	[fastest]
5. gracefully	[more/less gracefully]	[most/least gracefully]

B. On the line write the comparative form of the adverb at the left.

early 1. The day of the field trip we got up [earlier] than usual.

fast 2. Mercury spins on its axis [faster] than Venus does.

late 3. Our guests arrived [later] than we expected.

clearly 4. He speaks [more/less clearly] than he writes.

slowly 5. Please speak [more/less slowly].

C. On the line write the superlative form of the adverb at the left.

far 1. Andrew threw the Frisbee [farthest].

clearly 2. Of all the students in our class, Brice talks [most/least clearly].

fast 3. Marlene finished the assignment [fastest].

near 4. Melody is sitting [nearest] to the blackboard.

carefully 5. Of all the bus drivers, Mr. Pulaski drives [most/least carefully].

90

87. More Comparative and Superlative Adverbs

A. Circle the correct form of the adverb.

1. The bus left (later, latest) than we expected.

2. Doug cooks (more often, most often) than he used to.

3. Can you walk (faster, fastest) than that?

4. The bells rang (louder, loudest) than usual.

5. The last surfer rode the waves (more gracefully, most gracefully).

6. Please examine this fossil (more carefully, most carefully) of all.

7. Jason cooks (worse, worst) than Allen does.

8. Jonathan skated (more skillfully, most skillfully) than Bert did.

9. Marty works (more diligently, most diligently) of all the students.

10. You are making a lot of noise, Karen and Linda. Please work (more quietly, most quietly).

B. Complete each sentence with the correct form of the adverb.

closely　　1. We looked _____[more/less closely]_____ at the gems than at the other rock specimens in the exhibit.

easily　　2. Of all the math problems in the assignment, I solved this one _____[most/least easily]_____.

well　　3. The basketball team played _____[better/worse]_____ today than it did yesterday.

fast　　4. Please work _____[faster]_____.

clearly　　5. Kate was selected for the play because she speaks _____[more clearly]_____ than Cindy does.

violently　　6. The volcano erupted _____[more/less violently]_____ than it had in decades.

hard　　7. Because he had worked _____[hard]_____ all year, Tyrone was happy when summer vacation arrived.

politely　　8. Of all the clerks, Ms. Grimes deals with customers _____[most/least politely]_____.

softly　　9. Please play that music _____[more/less softly]_____.

rapid　　10. Express mail is delivered _____[more rapidly]_____ than regular mail.

88. Adverbs and Adjectives

An adjective describes a noun or a pronoun. It may precede or follow the word it describes, or it may follow a linking verb. An adverb modifies a verb, an adjective, or another adverb. An adverb may appear at various locations in a sentence.

NOUN   ADJECTIVE

That sound from the radio isn't really clear.

VERB   ADVERB

Actors must say their lines clearly.

Do not confuse the adjective *good* and the adverb *well*. The comparative form of both words is *better*, and the superlative of both is *best (good, better best; well, better, best)*.

Circle the correct word in parentheses. Write on the line whether the word is used as an adjective or an adverb.

[adjective] 1. During the Revolution, Tories were ((loyal) loyally) to Britain.

[adjective] 2. The crossing guard always looks ((cheerful) cheerfully) in the morning.

[adverb] 3. Rita plays the violin (good (well)).

[adjective] 4. The new bus driver seems quite ((capable) capably).

[adverb] 5. Please move that computer (careful (carefully)) so you don't drop it.

[adverb] 6. The child (forgetful (forgetfully)) left her toy on the lawn.

[adverb] 7. The teacher explained the math problems very (good (well)).

[adjective] 8. The oatmeal tasted ((delicious) deliciously).

[adjective] 9. This pink and orange sunset is really ((beautiful) beautifully).

[adjective] 10. Marcy is always ((thoughtful) thoughtfully) of others.

[adverb] 11. The students worked (quiet (quietly)) on their own.

[adverb] 12. Mrs. Lee (generous (generously)) donated a million dollars to charity.

[adjective] 13. The nurses in that hospital are very ((helpful) helpfully).

[adverb] 14. The director spoke (angry (angrily)) to the cast during rehearsals.

[adverb] 15. Margie (polite (politely)) thanked her grandmother for the gift.

Adverbs

89. Negative Words

Using two negative words where only one is needed is called a double negative. If a sentence already has a negative word, avoid using another negative word. The most common negative adverbs are *no, not,* and *never.* The adverbs *barely, hardly,* and *scarcely* have a negative sense and should not be used with other negative terms.

INCORRECT **Never eat no wild mushrooms.**

CORRECT **Never eat any wild mushrooms.**

INCORRECT **I can't hardly reach the top shelf.**

CORRECT **I can hardly reach the top shelf.**
I can't reach the top shelf.

A. Underline the correct word in parentheses.

1. There are things people should (never ever) do around the house.

2. Don't insert (any no) more than two plugs into one outlet.

3. Don't (ever never) stick a knife into a toaster that is plugged in.

4. Never run (any no) wires under a rug or carpet.

5. (Never Ever) touch an electrical wire with wet hands.

6. Don't (ever never) put your finger directly into an electrical outlet.

7. (No one Anyone) should use a power tool unless he or she is wearing safety glasses.

8. Don't leave (any no) toys or shoes on the stairs.

9. (Ever Never) keep household cleansers within reach of small children.

10. (Any No) sharp objects should be left where toddlers can find them.

B. Rewrite the following sentences to correct any errors in the use of negatives.
[Answers may vary.]

1. We couldn't barely move the heavy couch.

[We could barely move the heavy couch.]

2. She didn't have no way to get to the library.

[She had no way to get to the library.]

3. There's not scarcely enough time to finish.

[There's scarcely enough time to finish.]

4. I can't hardly read that sign.

[I can hardly read that sign.]

5. I haven't never any energy left.

[I never have any energy left.]

Adverbs

90. Adverb Phrases and Clauses

A **prepositional phrase** is made up of a preposition, its object, and any modifiers of the object. A prepositional phrase used as an adverb is an **adverb phrase**. Adverb phrases tell when, where, how, how much, why, or to what extent.

The children are playing <u>in the park</u>.

A **clause** is a group of words that has a subject and a predicate. A dependent clause cannot stand on its own as a sentence. A dependent clause used as an adverb is an **adverb clause**. An adverb clause answers the same questions as an adverb phrase.

They will come home <u>after they finish their game</u>.

A. Underline the adverb phrase in each sentence. Circle the word(s) it modifies.

1. Many American families (move) <u>during the summer</u>.

2. The children (will start) classes <u>in the fall</u>.

3. Some children (worry) <u>about their new schools</u>.

4. Many children (write) their worries <u>in their journals</u>.

5. As soon as possible, the children become (familiar) <u>with their new surroundings</u>.

6. They (may ride) their bikes <u>around their neighborhoods</u>.

7. They (research) their new cities <u>on the Internet</u>.

8. They (search) <u>online</u> <u>for local radio stations</u>.

9. They (learn) <u>about parks and community activities</u>.

10. They (leave) their e-mail addresses <u>with their old friends</u>.

B. Underline the adverb clause in each sentence. Circle the word(s) it modifies.

1. <u>Before we moved</u>, I (downloaded) a map of our new neighborhood.

2. I (drew) the route to school <u>so that I wouldn't get lost</u>.

3. <u>Since I belong to a scout troop</u>, I (contacted) a troop in my new town.

4. I (took) photos of my old room <u>because I want to remember it</u>.

5. I (bought) an autograph book <u>so that all my friends could sign it</u>.

6. <u>Whenever I feel sad</u>, I (read) what they wrote.

7. <u>While I was packing</u>, I (selected) toys to donate to charity.

8. <u>After the truck was loaded</u>, I (walked) around the neighborhood one last time.

9. I (will call) my friends <u>if I feel lonely</u>.

10. <u>Although they live in a different town</u>, I (know) how to contact them.

91. Reviewing Adverbs

A. Underline each adverb. Write on the line what it indicates—**T** for time, **P** for place, **M** for manner, **D** for degree, **A** for affirmation, or **N** for negation.

___[T]___ 1. We saw a great baseball game <u>recently</u>.

___[M]___ 2. Runners from the opposing team were on first and second bases, and we waited <u>anxiously</u> for the pitcher to throw the ball.

___[M]___ 3. Our pitcher threw the ball <u>hard</u>.

___[P]___ 4. The batter swung <u>low</u> and missed.

___[M]___ 5. The runner <u>unexpectedly</u> tried to steal third base.

___[N]___ 6. The runner did <u>not</u> make it. The catcher threw the ball to the player at <u>third</u> base, who tagged the runner.

___[M]___ 7. The fans jumped to their feet <u>excitedly</u>.

___[P]___ 8. I jumped <u>up</u> with the others!

___[D]___ 9. The crowd <u>really</u> cheered!

___[A]___ 10. <u>Yes</u>, our team held its lead!

B. Circle the correct adverb in parentheses. On the line write **C** if the adverb is comparative or **S** if it is superlative.

___[S]___ 11. Sound travels quickly. It travels (faster (fastest)) of all in solid materials.

___[C]___ 12. Sound travels ((more slowly) most slowly) through gases than through solid materials.

___[C]___ 13. Light travels ((more quickly) most quickly) than sound does.

___[C]___ 14. Light travels ((better) best) through a transparent solid like clear glass than through a translucent solid such as frosted glass.

___[S]___ 15. Compared with heat and sound, light travels through space (faster (fastest)).

C. Circle the correct word in parentheses. Write on the line whether it is an adjective or an adverb.

_____[adverb]_____ 16. Marta looked at the large package (hopeful (hopefully)).

_____[adjective]_____ 17. She was ((eager) eagerly) to see the contents.

_____[adverb]_____ 18. Her mother (careful (carefully)) opened the mysterious box.

_____[adverb]_____ 19. Marta waited (patient (patiently)) while her mother pulled out a present.

_____[adjective]_____ 20. Marta felt ((happy) happily) about the beautiful book her grandmother had sent her.

CONTINUED

Adverbs

D. Underline each adverb phrase. Circle the word(s) it modifies.

21. We (visited) many places on our trip.

22. We (drove) through Redwood National Park.

23. Many huge trees (grow) in this park.

24. Some trees (have lived) for centuries.

25. You (can) actually (drive) through one large tree.

E. Underline each adverb clause. Circle the word(s) it modifies.

26. Many people (went) to California after gold was discovered there.

27. Although some people found gold, others (made) money in different ways.

28. When Levi Strauss got there, he (made) pants for miners.

29. The miners (liked) the pants because they were strong and cheap.

30. Whenever you wear Levi's, you (should think) of Levi Strauss.

F. Circle the correct word in parentheses.

31. My friends have (ever (never)) been to California.

32. Has no one ((ever) never) visited a movie studio?

33. We didn't see ((any) no) movie stars when we were there.

34. There wasn't ((any) no) sight more impressive than the redwoods.

35. We had (ever (never)) seen such tall trees before.

Try It Yourself

Write three sentences about an exciting event that you attended or that you saw on TV. Be sure to use adverbs correctly.

_____

_____

_____

Check Your Own Work

Choose a selection from your writing portfolio, your journal, a work in progress, an assignment from another subject, or a letter. Revise it, applying the skills you have reviewed. This checklist will help you.

✔ Have you included appropriate adverbs of time, place, and manner?

✔ Have you used the correct form for adverbs used in comparisons?

✔ Have you used adverb forms, and not adjective forms, where they are needed?

✔ Have you followed the rules for avoiding double negatives?

Adverbs

Name _____

92. Simple Subjects and Simple Predicates

A sentence has a subject and a predicate. The **simple subject** is the noun or pronoun that names the person, place, or thing the sentence is about. The **simple predicate** is the verb that tells what the subject does or is.

SIMPLE SUBJECT	SIMPLE PREDICATE
Water	evaporates.
Cold water	evaporates slowly.
Water at the boiling point	evaporates quickly.

A. Write the simple subject and the simple predicate of each sentence in the appropriate column.

	SIMPLE SUBJECT	SIMPLE PREDICATE
1. Plants need water.	[Plants]	[need]
2. Plants in the desert get water in many ways.	[Plants]	[get]
3. A cactus stores water in its thick stem.	[cactus]	[stores]
4. Some plants have long roots.	[plants]	[have]
5. These long roots reach water deep underground.	[roots]	[reach]
6. Flowers bloom after a rainstorm.	[Flowers]	[bloom]
7. Animals need water too.	[Animals]	[need]
8. Many animals in the desert rest all day.	[animals]	[rest]
9. Foxes hunt in the cool evenings.	[Foxes]	[hunt]
10. The food of some animals provides them with water.	[food]	[provides]

B. Draw one line under the simple subject. Draw two lines under the simple predicate.

1. Animals in the ocean obtain oxygen and food from the water around them.

2. Some of these animals hunt for food.

3. Other kinds always stay in one place.

4. Microscopic animals in the water are an important source of food.

5. Whales filter these animals from seawater for food.

Name _____

93. Complete Subjects and Complete Predicates

> The **complete subject** of a sentence is the simple subject with all the words that describe it. The **complete predicate** contains the verb, its modifiers, and its complements or objects.
>
> COMPLETE SUBJECT
> **The islands of the West Indies**
>
> COMPLETE PREDICATE
> **lie between North and South America.**
>
> SIMPLE SUBJECT
> **islands**
>
> SIMPLE PREDICATE
> **lie**

Draw a vertical line between the complete subject and the complete predicate. Draw one line under the simple subject. Draw two lines under the simple predicate.

1. The West Indies | separate the Caribbean Sea from the Atlantic Ocean.

2. The chain of islands | is about 3,200 kilometers long.

3. The West Indies' climate | is tropical.

4. Destruction of the native forests | occurred during plantation days.

5. Sugar-plantation owners | needed wood for hot fires for sugar refining.

6. Some countries | passed laws to protect the forests.

7. The people of these islands | come from many parts of the world.

8. Languages spoken on the islands | include English, French, Spanish, and Dutch.

9. Many people on the islands | are descendants of slaves.

10. Caribbean countries | depend on farming for part of their income.

11. Farmers on these tropical islands | raise several different kinds of crops.

12. Exports from the islands | include sugar, bananas, and coffee.

13. The islands | import large amounts of wheat.

14. Tourism | brings a lot of business to the islands.

15. The island of Jamaica | is a popular tourist destination.

94. Compound Subjects and Compound Predicates

A **compound subject** consists of more than one simple subject.

> **Beatrix Potter** and **Beverly Cleary** are famous authors of children's books.

A **compound predicate** consists of more than one simple predicate.

> Their books **amuse** and **delight** children everywhere.

A. Each sentence has a compound subject or a compound predicate. Draw a vertical line between the subject and the predicate. Underline the compound subject or predicate.

1. The owl and the pussycat | went to sea in a beautiful pea-green boat.

2. The owl | looked up to the stars above and sang to a small guitar.

3. The walrus and the carpenter | were walking close at hand.

4. Jack and Jill | went up the hill for a pail of water.

5. Little Jack Horner | stuck in his thumb and pulled out a plum.

Sentences

B. Underline each compound subject. Circle each compound predicate.

1. Beatrix Potter (wrote) and (illustrated) her own stories.

2. Peter Rabbit and his family are the characters in one story.

3. Flopsy, Mopsy, and Cottontail lived with Peter under the root of a big fir tree.

4. Mr. McGregor and Mrs. McGregor (planted) and (weeded) their garden.

5. Mrs. Rabbit (shopped) for food and (cooked) the meals.

6. The four little bunnies (hopped) down the lane and (gathered) blackberries.

7. Mr. McGregor (shouted) and (waved) his rake.

8. Peter (ran) away and (squeezed) under the gate.

9. Flopsy, Mopsy, and Cottontail (ate) blackberries and (drank) milk.

10. Peter and his mother had tea for supper.

99

95. Natural and Inverted Order

A sentence is in **natural order** when the verb follows the subject.

SUBJECT VERB

The Spanish conquerors came onto the island.

A sentence is in **inverted order** when the verb or an auxiliary verb comes before the subject.

VERB SUBJECT

Onto the island came the Spanish conquerors.

VERB SUBJECT VERB

When did the Spanish conquerors come onto the island?

A. Underline the subject once and the verb twice. On the line write **N** if the sentence is in natural order or **I** if it is in inverted order.

___[N]___ 1. Europeans first came to the Americas in the 11th century.

___[I]___ 2. To the Americas came explorers, missionaries, and settlers.

___[N]___ 3. Spain conquered much of Mexico, Central America, and South America.

___[I]___ 4. In the rest of North America lived settlers from England and France.

___[N]___ 5. The newly arrived Europeans uprooted and destroyed the Native American civilizations.

___[I]___ 6. Westward pushed the North American pioneers.

___[I]___ 7. To reservations went Native Americans.

___[N]___ 8. The Cherokee traveled from Georgia to the West on a journey later called the Trail of Tears.

___[I]___ 9. Were the Sioux moved to reservations?

___[N]___ 10. Early settlers focused on their needs for more territory and not on the needs of the native people.

B. Five of the sentences in Part A are in inverted order. Rewrite them in natural order on the lines.

1. _____ [Explorers, missionaries, and settlers came to the Americas.] _____

2. _____ [Settlers from England and France lived in the rest of North America.] _____

3. _____ [The North American pioneers pushed westward.] _____

4. _____ [Native Americans went to reservations.] _____

5. _____ [The Sioux were moved to reservations.] _____

96. More Natural and Inverted Order

A. Rewrite each sentence, using inverted order.
Use inverted order in questions where indicated.

1. The game of baseball developed from an English game called rounders. *(question)*

   [Did the game of baseball develop from an English game called rounders?]

2. The annual All-Star Game began in 1933.

   [In 1933 began the annual All-Star Game.]

3. Wrigley Field, the home of the Chicago Cubs, is here.

   [Here is Wrigley Field, the home of the Chicago Cubs.]

4. The Baseball Hall of Fame stands in Cooperstown, New York.

   [In Cooperstown, New York, stands the Baseball Hall of Fame.]

5. Hank Aaron's bat is among the baseball relics in the hall. *(question)*

   [Is Hank Aaron's bat among the baseball relics

   in the hall?]

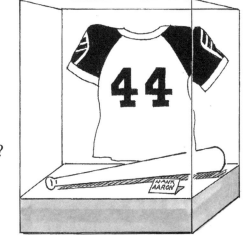

B. Rewrite each sentence, using natural order.
[Answers may vary.]

1. Does he know when the sport of baseball began?

   [He does know when the sport of baseball began.]

2. Named to the Baseball Hall of Fame in 1973
   was Roberto Clemente.

   [Roberto Clemente was named to the Baseball Hall of Fame in 1973.]

3. Into the air leapt the star outfielder.

   [The star outfielder leapt into the air.]

4. In the bottom of the ninth inning came the last desperate attempt to win.

   [The last desperate attempt to win came in the bottom of the ninth inning.]

5. Into home plate slid the runner with the winning run.

   [The runner slid into home plate with the winning run.]

97. Declarative Sentences and Interrogative Sentences

A **declarative sentence** makes a statement.
A declarative sentence ends with a period.

  A volcano is an opening in the earth's crust.

An **interrogative sentence** asks a question.
An interrogative sentence ends with a question mark.

  Why do volcanoes erupt?

On the line write whether each sentence is declarative
or interrogative. Add the correct end punctuation.

_____[declarative]_____ 1. Volcanoes have magma chambers inside them.

_____[interrogative]_____ 2. What is magma?

_____[declarative]_____ 3. Magma is molten rock.

_____[declarative]_____ 4. Volcanoes erupt because of density and pressure.

_____[interrogative]_____ 5. How does density affect a volcano?

_____[declarative]_____ 6. Magma is less dense than the surrounding rocks are.

_____[declarative]_____ 7. Bubbles of gas form in the magma.

_____[interrogative]_____ 8. What happens when the bubbles rise?

_____[declarative]_____ 9. The bubbles exert tremendous pressure on the rock.

_____[declarative]_____ 10. The pressure pushes the magma and rock out of the earth.

_____[interrogative]_____ 11. Is there molten rock on the surface of the earth?

_____[declarative]_____ 12. Lava is molten rock that reaches the earth's surface.

_____[declarative]_____ 13. In some volcanoes lava oozes out slowly.

_____[interrogative]_____ 14. Do some volcanoes explode violently?

_____[declarative]_____ 15. Rock, ash, and cinders can shoot out of openings.

_____[interrogative]_____ 16. How often do volcanoes erupt?

_____[declarative]_____ 17. Some volcanoes erupt more often than others.

_____[declarative]_____ 18. On average, Kilauea in Hawaii erupts every 3.95 years.

_____[declarative]_____ 19. Mount St. Helens in Washington state erupted in 1980.

_____[declarative]_____ 20. It hadn't erupted in more than 120 years.

Sentences

Name _____

98. Imperative Sentences and Exclamatory Sentences

An **imperative sentence** gives a command or makes a request.
An imperative sentence ends with a period.

> **Explain the nature of friction.**

An **exclamatory sentence** expresses a strong emotion.
An exclamatory sentence ends with an exclamation mark.

> **That's truly amazing!**

A. Underline the sentences that are imperative.

1. Friction makes moving in water difficult.
2. Take a smooth rubber ball and a tennis ball.
3. Put a little water into a shallow bowl.
4. Try spinning each ball in the bowl.
5. Which one spins more easily?
6. Write your results in your journal.
7. The rubber ball is smoother than the tennis ball.
8. The smooth surface causes less friction.
9. That's why a fast boat generally has a smooth body.
10. Think of another experiment dealing with friction.

B. On the line write whether each sentence is imperative or exclamatory.
Add the correct end punctuation. [**Some answers may vary.**]

____[imperative]____ 1. Get a glass jar with a lid.

____[imperative]____ 2. Have some soap and water ready.

____[imperative]____ 3. Screw the cover on the jar as tightly as you can.

____[exclamatory]____ 4. Be careful!

____[exclamatory]____ 5. Wow, that's really tight!

____[imperative]____ 6. Wet your hands with the soap and water.

____[imperative]____ 7. Try to take the lid off the jar.

____[exclamatory]____ 8. It's impossible!

____[imperative]____ 9. State an observation about friction.

____[exclamatory]____ 10. Think really hard!

99. The Four Kinds of Sentences

A sentence can be declarative, interrogative, imperative, or exclamatory.

On the line identify each sentence as declarative, interrogative, imperative, or exclamatory. Add the correct end punctuation. **[Some answers may vary.]**

_____[declarative]_____ 1. Irving Berlin was one of America's most successful songwriters.

_____[interrogative]_____ 2. Do you know the names of any of his songs?

_____[declarative]_____ 3. "White Christmas" and "God Bless America" are among his songs.

_____[declarative]_____ 4. Berlin couldn't read music or play the piano very well.

_____[exclamatory]_____ 5. That's incredible!

_____[declarative]_____ 6. During World War II Berlin wrote a musical about the army.

_____[imperative]_____ 7. Name the dates of World War II.

_____[declarative]_____ 8. The show raised about $10,000,000 for charity.

_____[exclamatory]_____ 9. That's what I call impressive!

_____[declarative]_____ 10. Berlin was born in Russia in 1888.

_____[interrogative]_____ 11. Why did the family move to the United States?

_____[declarative]_____ 12. There was discrimination against Jews in Russia.

_____[declarative]_____ 13. Berlin wrote many patriotic songs about America.

_____[interrogative]_____ 14. Can you sing one of his songs?

_____[imperative]_____ 15. Try to find out more about Irving Berlin.

Irving Berlin believed that music could cheer people up and give them courage. Give an example of how you can cheer people up and give them courage.

Sentences

Name _____

100. Simple Sentences

A **simple sentence** contains a subject and a predicate.
Either or both may be compound.

SUBJECT	PREDICATE
Lyndon Johnson	had a long record of public service.
Johnson and his wife, Lady Bird,	were from Texas.
Johnson	worked hard for civil rights laws and tried to help poor Americans.

Underline each simple subject once. Underline each simple
predicate twice. Identify each compound subject and
compound predicate by writing C in the appropriate column.

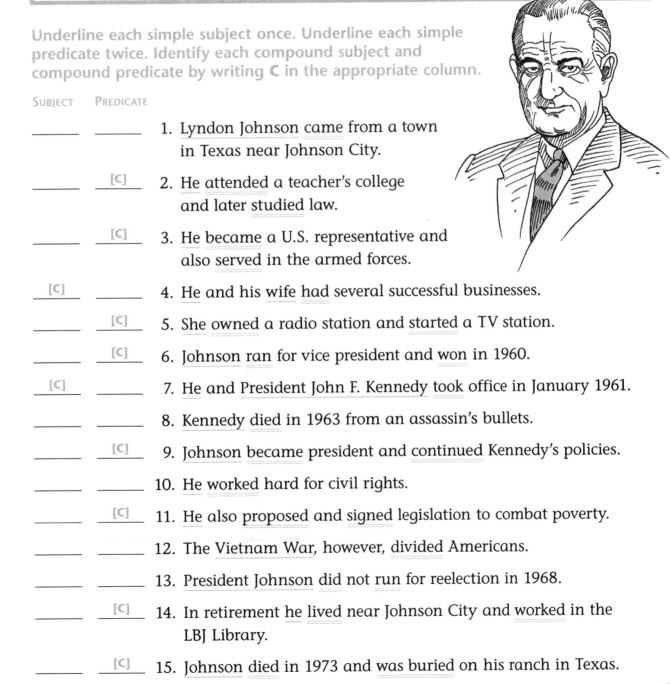

SUBJECT   PREDICATE

_____ _____ 1. Lyndon Johnson came from a town in Texas near Johnson City.

_____ [C] 2. He attended a teacher's college and later studied law.

_____ [C] 3. He became a U.S. representative and also served in the armed forces.

[C] _____ 4. He and his wife had several successful businesses.

_____ [C] 5. She owned a radio station and started a TV station.

_____ [C] 6. Johnson ran for vice president and won in 1960.

[C] _____ 7. He and President John F. Kennedy took office in January 1961.

_____ _____ 8. Kennedy died in 1963 from an assassin's bullets.

_____ [C] 9. Johnson became president and continued Kennedy's policies.

_____ _____ 10. He worked hard for civil rights.

_____ [C] 11. He also proposed and signed legislation to combat poverty.

_____ _____ 12. The Vietnam War, however, divided Americans.

_____ _____ 13. President Johnson did not run for reelection in 1968.

_____ [C] 14. In retirement he lived near Johnson City and worked in the LBJ Library.

_____ [C] 15. Johnson died in 1973 and was buried on his ranch in Texas.

101. Compound Sentences

A **compound sentence** contains two or more independent clauses.
An independent clause has a subject and a verb and can stand on
its own as a sentence. Independent clauses are usually connected by
the coordinating conjunctions *and, but, or, nor, yet,* and *so.*

INDEPENDENT CLAUSE   INDEPENDENT CLAUSE
Albany is the capital of New York, but New York City is its largest city.

Instead of a coordinating conjunction a semicolon may be used between
independent clauses.

Albany is the capital of New York; New York City is its largest city.

A. Underline the simple subjects once and the verbs twice. Circle the coordinating conjunction or the semicolon that connects the independent clauses.

1. New York City has the largest population of any city in the United States, (but) Los Angeles covers more land.

2. New York City is the largest city in the United States, (and) Los Angeles is the second largest.

3. New York City sits on a number of islands(;) the most famous island is Manhattan.

4. San Francisco is located in northern California, (and) Los Angeles is located in southern California.

5. Los Angeles has many TV and film studios, (and) San Francisco has a large computer industry.

6. San Francisco is fairly hilly(;) Los Angeles is more level.

7. Los Angeles and New York City are located on coasts(;) Chicago is inland.

8. New York City has many tall buildings, (but) Chicago has taller ones.

9. In Los Angeles many people drive to work, (and) in New York many people use subways.

10. Our family toured New York city last year, (but) I am anxious to visit it again.

B. On the line write **S** if the sentence is a simple sentence or **C** if the sentence is a compound sentence. Add the correct punctuation to each compound sentence.

___[S]___ 1. New York is famous for its large number of theaters.

___[C]___ 2. New York has several orchestras, and it has several ballet companies too.

___[C]___ 3. The Statue of Liberty is in New York Harbor; millions of people visit it yearly.

___[S]___ 4. New York City is a business center and is the home of many banks.

___[C]___ 5. The New York skyline is famous, and Central Park is a great escape from the hustle and bustle of the city.

102. More Compound Sentences

Combine each pair of simple sentences to form a compound sentence.
Use a comma before the coordinating conjunctions *and*, *but*, *or*, *nor*, *yet*, and *so*.
[Answers may vary.]

1. The United States celebrates its Independence Day on July 4. Peru celebrates
   its Independence Day on July 28.
   [The United States celebrates its Independence Day on July 4, and/but

   Peru celebrates its Independence Day on July 28.]

2. Americans might attend fireworks displays on July 4. They might stay
   home and watch them on TV.
   [Americans might attend fireworks displays on July 4, or they might stay

   home and watch them on TV.]

3. Many countries celebrate New Year's Day on January 1. In Muslim countries
   the new year begins on the first day of the month of Muharram.
   [Many countries celebrate New Year's Day on January 1, but in Muslim countries

   the new year begins on the first day of the month of Muharram.]

4. On New Year's Day many Americans attend football games or watch them on TV.
   On that day many Chinese visit friends and exchange gifts.
   [On New Year's Day many Americans attend football games or watch them on TV, but on that

   day many Chinese visit friends and exchange gifts.]

5. In the United States Mother's Day is in May. Father's Day is in June.
   [In the United States Mother's Day is in May, and Father's Day is in June.]

6. Carnival in Brazil is right before Lent. Mardi Gras in New Orleans is at the same time.
   [Carnival in Brazil is right before Lent, and Mardi Gras in New Orleans is at the same time.]

7. In most western countries Sunday is a holiday. In Islamic countries Friday
   is a holiday.
   [In most western countries Sunday is a holiday, and/but in Islamic countries Friday

   is a holiday.]

8. Queen Elizabeth's real birthday is April 21. People celebrate her birthday on the
   third Saturday in June, when the weather in England is pleasant.
   [Queen Elizabeth's real birthday is April 21, but people celebrate her birthday

   on the third Saturday in June, when the weather in England is pleasant.]

9. The birthday of the Queen of England is a holiday in England. This day is not
   a holiday in the United States.
   [The birthday of the Queen of England is a holiday in England, but this day is not a holiday

   in the United States.]

10. The Christian holiday of Easter is usually in April. Sometimes it is in March.
    [The Christian holiday of Easter is usually in April, but/and sometimes it is in March.]

Sentences

103. Reviewing Simple and Compound Sentences

On the line write **S** if a sentence is simple or **C** if it is compound.

___[C]___ 1. Fairy tales are fictitious, but they are excellent stories.

___[S]___ 2. In Germany the Grimm Brothers collected many fairy tales.

___[C]___ 3. Jacob Grimm was born in 1785, and Wilhelm Grimm was born in 1786.

___[S]___ 4. Jacob and Wilhelm at first studied law in college.

___[C]___ 5. They developed a love of German folk traditions from their teachers, and they began to study folktales and fairy stories.

___[C]___ 6. Many of these stories were quite old; some dated from the Middle Ages and earlier.

___[C]___ 7. The brothers became lawyers, but they remained interested in these stories.

___[S]___ 8. By 1814 they had given up their legal careers and were pursuing their studies of folktales.

___[C]___ 9. They did not make much money, and they had to spend their earnings carefully.

___[S]___ 10. They collected large numbers of stories and published them in a book.

___[S]___ 11. Some of the stories in their collection are versions of the Cinderella tale and the Rapunzel tale.

___[C]___ 12. This book was popular, and thousands of people bought copies.

___[S]___ 13. In 1840 the king of Prussia invited the brothers to Berlin.

___[C]___ 14. In Berlin the king paid them a generous salary, and they could focus on their work.

___[S]___ 15. Wilhelm and Jacob also began to study linguistics and published an important book about the German language.

___[C]___ 16. They also started work on a German dictionary, but the task was too large for them.

___[C]___ 17. Wilhelm finished only to the letter D by the time of his death, and Jacob reached only F.

___[S]___ 18. Their collections of stories and their other books made the brothers famous.

___[S]___ 19. They received prizes and honors.

___[S]___ 20. They are most beloved for their collections of fairy stories and folktales.

Sentences

Name _____

104. Prepositions

A **preposition** is a word that shows the relation of a noun or a pronoun to another word in a sentence. The noun or pronoun that follows the preposition is the **object of the preposition**.

PREPOSITION   OBJECT

Frederick Douglass made many contributions   to   the country.

Common prepositions are *at, after, against, by, for, from, in, into, of, on, to, with,* and *without.*

Circle each preposition.

1. Frederick Douglass was one of the most important human rights leaders of the 19th century.

2. He was born into slavery in Maryland with the name Frederick Bailey.

3. Shortly after his birth, his owners separated him from his mother, who was a slave.

4. His mother was moved some 20 miles away, a long distance in those days.

5. When he was seven or eight years old, his owner had him work for the Auld family in Baltimore.

6. At that time he learned reading from Mrs. Auld.

7. When children in the neighborhood finished their books, they gave them to young Frederick.

8. Against all odds Frederick continued teaching himself.

9. When he was older, Frederick escaped on a train, and he lived in New York as a free person.

10. He changed his name to Douglass.

11. Douglass began speaking against slavery.

12. He became a consultant to President Abraham Lincoln.

13. He helped convince Lincoln that slaves should be freed if they fought in the Civil War against the South.

14. After the war Douglass pressed for full civil rights for freed slaves.

15. Frederick Douglass became the first African American diplomat when he was appointed U.S. ambassador to Haiti.

Frederick Douglass worked hard to educate himself and then used his education to help others. Give an example of how you can use your education to help others.

105. Prepositional Phrases

A **prepositional phrase** consists of a preposition, a noun or a pronoun
that is its object, and any modifiers of the object.

The Missouri River is the longest river <u>in the United States</u>.

A. Underline each prepositional phrase. Circle each preposition.

1. The Mississippi River starts (in) Minnesota (near) the Canadian border.

2. It flows (toward) the south.

3. South (of) St. Paul, Minnesota, the river becomes wide enough and deep enough
   (for) vessels.

4. Two major tributaries, the Missouri River and the Ohio River, flow (into) it.

5. The Missouri River joins the Mississippi River (at) St. Louis.

6. After the river is joined (by) the Ohio River, it becomes huge.

7. (In) many places, the river is a mile and a half (from) shore (to) shore.

8. This river is one (of) the busiest commercial waterways (in) the world.

9. The river floods (in) spring, which often causes damage (to) cities (near) the river.

10. The Mississippi empties (into) the Gulf (of) Mexico (through) a huge delta.

B. Use each preposition in a prepositional phrase about a body of water near your
home. Circle the object of the preposition. **[Answers will vary. Sample answers are given.]**

1. through _____ [the muddy (water)] _____

2. near _____ [the (shore)] _____

3. from _____ [our (canoe)] _____

4. over _____ [the shining (surface)] _____

5. into _____ [the cold lake (water)] _____

C. Write a sentence, using each phrase from Part B.
[Sentences will vary. Sample sentences are given.]

1. [We pulled the oars through the muddy water.] _____

2. [Near the shore were several other boats.] _____

3. [Taking pictures from our canoe was quite difficult.] _____

4. [As we moved over the shining surface, the canoe tipped.] _____

5. [Some supplies fell into the cold lake water.] _____

Sentences

106. At and To, Between and Among

> *At* shows presence in. *To* shows motion toward.
>
> **Ed and Bert are at the museum. They're going to the gold exhibit.**
>
> Use *between* to speak of two persons, places, or things.
> Use *among* to speak of more than two.
>
> **There is much trade between the United States and Canada.**
> **There is trade among the United States, Canada, and Mexico.**

A. Complete each sentence with *at* or *to*.

1. Our class took a trip __[to]__ New York.

2. We spent the morning __[at]__ the
   United Nations (UN) headquarters.

3. We sailed __[to]__ the Statue of Liberty.

4. We stood __[at]__ the foot of the statue.

5. Then we walked __[to]__ the top.

6. After that we went __[to]__ Ellis Island.

7. Many immigrants __[to]__ the United States arrived at Ellis Island.

8. We also went __[to]__ the Metropolitan Museum of Art.

9. We saw many important exhibits __[at]__ the museum.

10. We also saw animals __[at]__ the zoo in Central Park.

B. Complete each sentence with *between* or *among*.

1. The United Nations works for peace __[among]__ all the countries
   of the world.

2. The treaty written by the North Atlantic Treaty Organization (NATO)
   is an agreement __[among]__ various Western powers.

3. It was signed during the cold war __[between]__ the East and the West.

4. Trade __[between]__ the United States and Mexico has been increasing.

5. The United States wants to increase trade __[among]__ all countries
   of North America and South America.

Sentences

107. Beside and Besides, In and Into

Beside means "at the side of" or "next to."
Besides means "in addition to" or "except."

> **The driver stood beside his car.**
> **Seven students besides me are in the tennis class.**

Use *in* to show location within something.
Use *into* to show motion toward a place or a change of location.

> **Rabbits live in burrows.**
> **If a rabbit is surprised, it will run into its burrow.**

A. Circle the correct preposition.

1. The jockey stood (**beside** besides) her horse, Holly's Hope.

2. There are seven horses in the race (**besides** beside) Holly's Hope.

3. What kind of ice cream do you like (**besides** beside) strawberry?

4. I don't like any flavor (beside **besides**) mint.

5. Our class planted a tree (**beside** besides) the school building.

6. (**Besides** Beside) the tree we also hope to buy and plant a rose bush.

7. (Beside **Besides**) the gorilla the snow leopard is an endangered species.

8. The naturalist sat right (**beside** besides) the gorilla in the wild.

9. Three students (**besides** beside) Jeanette are absent today.

10. The girl who sits (besides **beside**) me is a new student.

B. Circle the correct preposition.

1. The diver put on a wetsuit and jumped (in **into**) the water.

2. The diver went (**into** in) a large underwater coral reef.

3. The diver saw many unusual creatures (into **in**) the reef.

4. Many of the reef's inhabitants live (**in** into) colorful shells.

5. Small fish swim (**into** in) crevices in the reef if a predator is near.

6. They will hide (**in** into) the crevices until the danger is past.

7. The diver shined a light (**into** in) a crevice.

8. He saw a number of fish (into **in**) the darkness.

9. A small shark sometimes swims (in **into**) a coral reef.

10. All the other fish hide (**in** into) safe places until the shark goes away.

Sentences

Name _____

108. Prepositions and Adverbs

A preposition shows a relationship between its object and some other word in the sentence. An adverb tells how, when, or where. Many words can be used as prepositions or as adverbs.

PREPOSITION

Help is available to the flood victims <u>through</u> the Red Cross.

ADVERB

Because of the flood, trains could not get <u>through</u>.

A. On the line write **P** if the *italicized* word is a preposition or **A** if it is an adverb.

___[A]___ 1. Please open the door and come *in*.

___[P]___ 2. A large fire was burning *in* the fireplace.

___[P]___ 3. The coffee shop *across* the street opens at 6 a.m.

___[A]___ 4. Our teacher always gets his ideas *across* clearly.

___[A]___ 5. Rex, my dog, is always *near* when I'm home.

___[P]___ 6. Rex's bed is *near* the back door.

___[A]___ 7. Please put that box *down* in the kitchen.

___[P]___ 8. The kitchen is *down* those stairs.

___[P]___ 9. There was helium *inside* the balloon.

___[A]___ 10. On cold days I stay *inside* and work on my computer.

B. Write a sentence, using each adverb and each prepositional phrase. [Answers will vary. Sample sentences are given.]

outside *(adverb)*   1. _____[The children played outside this afternoon.]_____

outside the door   2. _____[They left their boots outside the door.]_____

up *(adverb)*   3. _____[We looked up when we heard the helicopter.]_____

up the stairs   4. _____[As I went up the stairs, I struggled with the heavy box.]_____

past *(adverb)*   5. _____[When you near the haunted house, just hurry past.]_____

past the house   6. _____[Danny has gone past the house many times.]_____

through *(adverb)*   7. _____[I hadn't gone through, so Danny insisted we do so.]_____

through the door   8. _____[I heard creaking sounds through the door.]_____

in *(adverb)*   9. _____[After we got in, I tried to leave as soon as possible.]_____

in the garden   10. _____[Even in the garden there were eerie shapes and shadows.]_____

Name _____

109. Adjective Phrases

> An **adjective phrase** is a prepositional phrase used as an adjective.
> **I read an article about the environment.**

A. Underline each adjective phrase.
Circle the noun each modifies.

1. (Bees) from Africa, called Africanized bees or killer bees, are invading the Americas.

2. (People) in Brazil originally brought them to the Western Hemisphere.

3. They wanted an (increase) in honey production.

4. The (spread) of the bees is occurring gradually.

5. (Areas) of Texas, New Mexico, Arizona, and California now have these bees.

6. The bees are fierce (defenders) of their nests.

7. They will immediately attack any nearby (source) of movement.

8. Numerous bees might join together and make an (attack) on a person.

9. One (defense) against these bees is running for shelter.

10. (Pursuit) by the bees, however, can continue up to a mile!

B. Rewrite each group of words as an adjective phrase. [Answers will vary.]

Example: arrival time   time of arrival

United States flag	1.	[flag of the United States]
children's drawings	2.	[drawings by children]
forest animals	3.	[animals of the forest]
wolf's den	4.	[den of the wolf]
animal's tracks	5.	[tracks of the animal]
house plants	6.	[plants in the house]
jungle adventures	7.	[adventures in the jungle]
leopard's spots	8.	[spots of the leopard]
soccer rules	9.	[rules of soccer]
piano keys	10.	[keys of the piano]

Sentences

114

110. More Adjective Phrases

A. Use the noun at the left to write an adjective phrase to complete each sentence.
[Answers will vary. Sample answers are given.]

distance   1. That mountain _____ [in the distance] _____ is Pike's Peak.

courage   2. The world will always need leaders _____ [with courage] _____.

Brazil   3. Coffee _____ [from Brazil] _____ is shipped to the
               United States.

ice   4. The sidewalk glistened in its coat _____ [of ice] _____.

California 5. Film studios _____ [of/in California] _____ are where many movies
               are made.

intelligence 6. Eleanor Roosevelt was a woman _____ [of/with great intelligence] _____.

France   7. The United States asked the government
               _____ [of France] _____ for help.

strength   8. Only a person _____ [with strength] _____
               could move this piano alone.

fear   9. This assignment requires a soldier
               _____ [without fear] _____.

Poland   10. The flight _____ [to/for/from Poland] _____
               took off at 10:00 this morning.

B. Complete each sentence with an adjective phrase.
[Answers will vary. Samples are given.]

1. The fire _____ [in the warehouse] _____ caused a great deal of damage.

2. The cheers _____ [of the crowd] _____ filled the theater.

3. Hugh is the best player _____ [on the basketball team] _____.

4. The president _____ [of the United States] _____ gave a report to Congress.

5. The flowers _____ [in the centerpiece] _____ are beautifully arranged.

6. The road _____ [to my friend's house] _____ is quite narrow.

7. The door _____ [near the fire escape] _____ is open.

8. The principal _____ [of our school] _____ made an announcement.

9. The Bill of Rights guarantees freedom _____ [of speech] _____.

10. The food _____ [from the deli] _____ was delicious.

111. Adverb Phrases

> An **adverb phrase** is a prepositional phrase used as an adverb.
> The United States and Canada are located <u>in North America</u>.

A. Underline each adverb phrase.

1. Buffalo once roamed <u>over the Great Plains</u>.

2. Corn and wheat grow <u>in the Midwest</u>.

3. The Ohio and Missouri Rivers flow <u>into the Mississippi River</u>.

4. Many large cities lie <u>along these rivers</u>.

5. The eastern rim of the plains is formed <u>by the Appalachian Mountains</u>.

6. <u>Across the plains</u> the Rockies and the Sierra Nevadas form the western boundary.

7. Settlers crossed the Great Plains <u>in covered wagons</u>.

8. They built towns <u>in valleys</u> and <u>along rivers</u>.

9. They often lived <u>in simple log cabins</u>.

10. Pioneers sometimes encountered danger <u>in their new homes</u>.

11. Wolves and bears often lived <u>in nearby forests</u>.

12. Settlers farmed <u>during the summer</u>.

13. <u>In the winter</u> they cleared land.

14. Early settlers built towns <u>across the plains</u>.

15. Look <u>on a map</u> and find these locations.

B. Write sentences, replacing the *italicized* adverb with an adverb phrase.
[Sentences will vary.]

lived *peacefully*   1. _____ [Pioneers generally lived in peace.] _____

moved *westward*   2. _____ [The settlers moved to/toward the west.] _____

grew *swiftly*   3. _____ [Some areas grew with swiftness.] _____

drove *carefully*   4. _____ [Coachmen drove with care as they steered the stagecoaches.] _____

listened *silently*   5. _____ [Travelers listened in silence as storms approached.] _____

Name _____

112. More Adverb Phrases

A. Complete each sentence with an adverb phrase. [Answers will vary. Sample answers are given.]

1. The audience laughed _____ [during the clown's performance] _____ .

2. _____ [On Sundays] _____ our family visits my grandmother.

3. The airplane landed _____ [on the runway] _____ .

4. Can you be ready _____ [by seven o'clock] _____ ?

5. Yesterday afternoon they played ball _____ [at Leahy Park] _____ .

6. Kelly lost her backpack _____ [on the playground] _____ .

7. I put the candy _____ [into the candy dish] _____ .

8. Flowers grow _____ [in bright sunlight] _____ .

9. I sometimes watch TV _____ [after school] _____ .

10. He parked the car _____ [near the curb] _____ .

11. We ate lunch _____ [in the cafeteria] _____ .

12. The teacher collected the papers _____ [after class] _____ .

13. A fire truck drove up _____ [to the store] _____ .

14. Please put the dishes away _____ [in the cabinet] _____ .

15. Hang your coat _____ [on that clothes rack] _____ .

B. Use each adverb phrase in a sentence. [Sentences will vary. Sample answers are given.]

at all times   1. _____ [Be careful at all times.] _____

in the park   2. _____ [We can meet in the park.] _____

at five o'clock   3. _____ [Generally, dinner is served at five o'clock.] _____

in the living room   4. _____ [The puppy should not be in the living room.] _____

at school   5. _____ [How many times have you left your gloves at school?] _____

Sentences

117

113. Complex Sentences, Adverb Clauses

A **complex sentence** contains an independent clause and one or more dependent clauses. An independent clause has a subject and a verb and can stand alone as a sentence. A dependent clause has a subject and a verb but cannot stand alone as a sentence. A dependent clause usually begins with a **subordinate conjunction**, such as *although, after, because, before, if, provided that, since, so that, unless, until,* or *when.* One type of dependent clause is an **adverb clause.** An adverb clause acts as an adverb and modifies a verb, an adjective, or another adverb.

INDEPENDENT CLAUSE   DEPENDENT CLAUSE

**The Eiffel Tower was the
world's tallest structure**   **when it opened in 1889.**

A. On the line write **I** if the clause is independent or **D** if it is dependent.

___[I]___ 1. some people thought the tower was an eyesore

___[D]___ 2. because birds might fly into it

___[D]___ 3. although many taller structures have been built

___[I]___ 4. the designer was Alexandre Gustave Eiffel

___[D]___ 5. before the tower was completed

___[I]___ 6. from the top it is possible to see 40 miles in every direction

___[I]___ 7. the two restaurants within the tower offer great views of Paris

___[D]___ 8. unless the day is overcast

___[D]___ 9. while the tower was being constructed

___[D]___ 10. as there is a Web cam on the top of the tower

B. Underline the adverb clause in each sentence. Circle the word(s) it modifies.

1. Before construction of the tower began, people (thought) it would cost too much.

2. The tower (was completed) under budget because the crew was so efficient.

3. Although the tower is very tall, it (does) not (sway) much in the wind.

4. Eiffel (designed) the tower so that the wind could blow through it.

5. Since weather erodes the paint, the tower (is painted) brown every seven years.

6. Until the tower opened, there (were) few tall structures with elevators.

7. Unless you are prepared to climb about 1,700 steps, you (should take) an elevator.

8. (Because) the tower is illuminated, tourists can see its steelwork even at night.

9. Although it is twice as tall as the Washington Monument, it (weighs) much less.

10. More than 200 million people (have visited) the tower since it opened.

114. Reviewing Sentences

A. Indicate how each *italicized* phrase is used. On the line write **Adj** if it is used as an adjective or **Adv** if it is used as an adverb.

[Adv] 1. The common cold can be caused *by many different viruses*.

[Adv] 2. Usually a cold virus is caught *from another person*.

[Adj] 3. Infections *in the throat* can lead to coughs.

[Adj] 4. Cough medicine can reduce the amount *of discomfort* a person experiences.

[Adj] 5. So far no one has invented an actual cure *for the common cold*.

B. Underline each simple subject once. Underline each simple predicate twice. A subject or a predicate may be compound.

6. Microbes grow or multiply on most foods.

7. Is the infection or disease bacterial or viral?

8. The conditions and requirements for their growth vary.

9. Warmth, moisture, and a source of food are necessary to most organisms.

10. In the kitchen, microbes can cause food poisoning.

11. A few steps can reduce or eliminate the chances of poisoning.

12. Meat and poultry should be stored properly and cooked completely.

13. People should refrigerate leftover food promptly.

14. Everyone should wash his or her hands before cooking or eating.

15. People should also wash dishes in hot, soapy water.

C. On the line write **S** if a sentence is simple or **C** if it is compound.

_[C]_ 16. Nutrients give you energy, and they are essential for growth and good health.

_[S]_ 17. Select foods from a variety of food groups.

_[C]_ 18. Fats give your body energy, but protein builds and repairs.

_[S]_ 19. Oranges and grapefruit are excellent sources of vitamin C.

_[S]_ 20. Milk and milk products such as yogurt and cheese supply calcium, protein, and several vitamins.

Sentences

119

D. On the line write **N** if the sentence is in natural order or **I** if it is in inverted order. Then rewrite the sentence to change its order. [Answers may vary.]

___[I]___ 21. Did he hear about the swim meet at the park yesterday?

        [He did hear about the swim meet at the park yesterday.]

___[N]___ 22. Children from all over the city competed in the meet.

        [In the meet competed children from all over the city.]

___[I]___ 23. Awarded the first prize was Elena Hernandez.

        [Elena Hernandez was awarded the first prize.]

___[I]___ 24. Onto the winner's podium stepped a smiling Elena.

        [A smiling Elena stepped onto the winner's podium.]

___[I]___ 25. Will Elena compete in the citywide meet next month?

        [Elena will compete in the

        citywide meet next month.]

Try It Yourself

Write four sentences about your favorite book or folktale.
Be sure to use various types of phrases, clauses, and sentences correctly.

_____

_____

_____

_____

Check Your Own Work

Choose a selection from your writing portfolio, your journal,
a work in progress, an assignment from another subject, or a letter.
Revise it, applying the skills you have reviewed. This checklist will help you.

✔ Have you chosen adjective and adverb phrases that add detail to your descriptions?

✔ Have you corrected any incomplete sentences?

✔ Have you used conjunctions, commas, and semicolons correctly to join compound sentences?

Sentences

Name _____

115. Conjunctions Connecting Words

> A **conjunction** is a word used to connect words, phrases, or clauses in a sentence. A **coordinating conjunction** connects similar words or groups of words; it connects words that have the same use in a sentence. These words may be nouns, verbs, adjectives, or adverbs. The coordinating conjunctions are *and, but, or, nor,* and *yet.*
>
> **Canadians can watch U.S. TV shows or Canadian TV shows.** *(nouns)*
> **Canada is large but relatively sparse in population.** *(adjectives)*
> **The Canadian hockey team skated quickly and expertly.** *(adverbs)*

A. Circle each conjunction. Underline the words it connects.

1. Two of Canada's most important industries are mining and manufacturing.

2. Lakes and streams are abundant in northwestern Canada.

3. Manitoba and Ontario are two Canadian provinces.

4. In parts of Canada you may hear English or French spoken.

5. Many Canadians' first language is not English but French.

6. A passport or proof of U.S. citizenship is required for people traveling between Canada and the United States.

7. The Alaska Highway, a 1,523-mile road, connects Dawson Creek in British Columbia and Fairbanks in Alaska.

8. The Great Lakes are in Canada and the United States.

9. Queen Elizabeth II of England is the head of state and monarch of Canada.

10. The preferred term for the Native Americans of northern Canada is not Eskimo but Inuit.

B. Complete each sentence with words connected by the conjunction.
[Answers will vary.]

1. _____ and _____ are states that border my state.

2. My favorite subjects in school are _____ and _____.

3. Today I feel _____ but _____.

4. Tonight I may watch _____ or _____ on TV.

5. My favorite foods are _____ and _____.

116. Conjunctions Connecting Prepositional Phrases

> Coordinating conjunctions can connect prepositional phrases.
> **Many different holidays are celebrated with fireworks and with parades.**

A. Circle each conjunction. Underline the phrases it connects.

1. On July 14, Bastille Day is celebrated in France (and) in its territories.
2. France's independence day is celebrated with dancing (and) with fireworks.
3. Soldiers on foot (and) in military vehicles parade down Paris streets.
4. Dragon Boat Festival in China is also known as Fifth Moon Festival (or) as Upright Sun Festival.
5. People race long boats with dragon-head fronts (and) with twisting dragon tails.
6. Cinco de Mayo is celebrated in Mexico (and) in many U.S. communities.
7. It marks Mexico's victory over the French (and) over France's colonial ambitions.
8. Street fairs with parades (and) with folk dancing are held throughout Mexico.
9. Citizenship Day on September 17 gives honor to native U.S. citizens (and) to naturalized citizens.
10. On September 28 Confucius's birthday is celebrated in China (and) by Confucius's followers elsewhere.
11. Lectures on his philosophy (and) about his life are presented.
12. On Earth Day, in April, people learn about the environment (and) about pollution.
13. People ride to work (or) to school on bicycles.
14. They are urged to think about conservation (and) about recycling.
15. Information on commemorative days is available on the Internet (and) from print sources such as books and magazines.

B. Write sentences with the following prepositional phrases. [Sentences will vary.]

1. with music and with dances

_____

2. on the street and in the home

_____

3. in Mexico and in the United States

_____

4. during the afternoon and at night

_____

5. with special foods and with gifts

_____

117. Conjunctions Connecting Clauses

Coordinating conjunctions can connect independent clauses or dependent clauses. When a coordinating conjunction joins independent clauses, a comma is used before the conjunction.

Most crocodiles live in fresh water, but some crocodiles live in salt water.

A. Circle each conjunction.
Underline the clauses it connects.

1. Crocodiles are in a group called crocodilians, (and) alligators belong to the same group.

2. Crocodiles have a protruding tooth, (but) alligators do not have one.

3. The snout of an alligator is broad, (but) the snout of a crocodile is narrow.

4. Both animals live in the southeastern part of the United States, (and) they are found in swamps and on river banks.

5. Alligators rest during the day, (and) they hunt at night.

6. They may float below the surface, (or) they may rest in a hole on a bank.

7. Crocodiles eat small aquatic animals, (but) they sometimes attack large mammals.

8. Alligators usually do not attack humans except in self-defense, (but) large crocodiles have been known to try to eat humans.

9. Alligators were in danger of extinction, (but) now laws protect them.

10. Alligators have been saved from extinction, (and) their numbers have increased.

B. Combine each pair of sentences with an appropriate coordinating conjunction.
[Answers may vary.]

1. Alligators live in the Southeast. They don't live in the West.
   [Alligators live in the Southeast, but they don't live in the West.]

2. Alligators were hunted for their skins. The skins were used for clothing.
   [Alligators were hunted for their skins, and the skins were used for clothing.]

3. People tried to save the alligators. Their efforts were successful.
   [People tried to save the alligators, and their efforts were successful.]

4. Laws were passed to limit hunting. These laws were effective.
   [Laws were passed to limit hunting, and these laws were effective.]

5. Some people are afraid of alligators. Alligators seldom attack humans.
   [Some people are afraid of alligators, but alligators seldom attack humans.]

Conjunctions, Interjections, Punctuation, Capitalization

118. Reviewing Conjunctions

Underline each conjunction. Write on the line whether it connects words, phrases, or clauses.

_____[words]_____ 1. Edward played <u>and</u> sang.

_____[phrases]_____ 2. Seeds are sown by hand <u>or</u> by machine.

_____[clauses]_____ 3. You can take the bus, <u>or</u> you can take the train.

_____[words]_____ 4. The coldest months are January <u>and</u> February.

_____[words]_____ 5. Lewis <u>and</u> Clark explored the western United States.

_____[clauses]_____ 6. Gloria bought the candy, <u>but</u> Ken ate it.

_____[words]_____ 7. My mother speaks English <u>and</u> Spanish fluently.

_____[phrases]_____ 8. The fox ran under the hedge <u>and</u> into the field.

_____[words]_____ 9. Maryland <u>and</u> Virginia gave land for the U.S. capital.

_____[phrases]_____ 10. These houses are for sale <u>or</u> for rent.

_____[clauses]_____ 11. The morning was rainy, <u>but</u> the afternoon was sunny.

_____[words]_____ 12. Broccoli <u>and</u> cauliflower are delicious.

_____[clauses]_____ 13. He ate one sundae, <u>and</u> he ordered another one.

_____[phrases]_____ 14. The jelly is on the table <u>or</u> in the refrigerator.

_____[words]_____ 15. Some airlines offer music <u>and</u> movies.

_____[clauses]_____ 16. Kate made a skirt, <u>and</u> Elaine knitted a sweater.

_____[words]_____ 17. Norway <u>and</u> Sweden are alike in several ways.

_____[clauses]_____ 18. Peter shook the tree, <u>and</u> an apple fell to the ground.

_____[clauses]_____ 19. Take the expressway, <u>and</u> you will arrive sooner.

_____[words]_____ 20. Skiing <u>and</u> snowboarding are winter sports.

119. Interjections

An **interjection** is a word that expresses a strong or sudden emotion. Interjections may express happiness, disgust, pain, agreement, impatience, surprise, sadness, amazement, and so on.

Oh, no! The baby spilled a whole box of cereal on the floor!
Wow! Tito Lopez is performing in our town this week.

Underline the interjections. Write on the line what feeling or emotion each interjection expresses.
[Answers will vary.]

_____ 1. Look! It's a family of bears.

_____ 2. He likes to eat fried pickles. Gross!

_____ 3. Oh, no! The test is today.

_____ 4. Hush! The president is about to speak!

_____ 5. Good! That was a great answer!

_____ 6. Today is Friday! Hooray!

_____ 7. You have a new cell phone? Great!

_____ 8. Oops! I dropped my sandwich.

_____ 9. Ouch! That plate is hot.

_____ 10. Oh! So that's how you turn on this computer.

_____ 11. Wow! That shirt is really expensive.

_____ 12. Oh, dear! It's raining cats and dogs, and I forgot my umbrella again.

_____ 13. We're having pizza for lunch. Yum!

_____ 14. Yes! Our team won the city championship.

_____ 15. Wonderful! We're going to the mall this afternoon.

_____ 16. Hey! Put that back.

_____ 17. No! You can't be serious.

_____ 18. Pavarotti sings on this CD. Excellent! I love his voice.

_____ 19. Oh, my! That sure costs a lot of money.

_____ 20. You'll be receiving a scholarship. How great!

120. Parts of Speech—Part I

On the line describe each *italicized* word as a noun, pronoun, verb, adjective, adverb, preposition, conjunction, or interjection.

_____[verb]_____ 1. Eleanor Roosevelt *was* one of the most admired and influential first ladies of the United States.

_____[adjective]_____ 2. She was born into a *wealthy* New York family that placed great value on education and public service.

_____[adverb]_____ 3. She studied in England and later worked *hard* as a teacher in a welfare center on New York's Lower East Side.

_____[conjunction]_____ 4. In 1905 she married Franklin Roosevelt *and* helped him in his career as a New York politician.

_____[noun]_____ 5. Her husband became *governor* of New York.

_____[adverb]_____ 6. After Franklin Roosevelt became president of the United States, she took a *very* active role.

_____[preposition]_____ 7. The country was suffering *from* the effects of the Great Depression of 1929, and many people were out of work.

_____[adjective]_____ 8. Living conditions for many Americans were *difficult*.

_____[conjunction]_____ 9. Mrs. Roosevelt visited the poor *and* reported on conditions to her husband.

_____[pronoun]_____ 10. *She* visited miners, farmers, and factory workers in every part of the country.

_____[adjective]_____ 11. She also worked hard to win *equal* rights for women and minorities.

_____[adverb]_____ 12. For example, Marian Anderson, an African American opera singer, was *not* allowed to sing in a Washington, D.C., concert hall.

_____[pronoun]_____ 13. Mrs. Roosevelt organized a concert for *her* at the Lincoln Memorial.

_____[noun]_____ 14. After President Roosevelt died in office in 1945, President Harry S Truman named Mrs. Roosevelt the U.S. *representative* to the United Nations.

_____[interjection]_____ 15. She continued to work for human rights until her death in 1962. *Wonderful!*

Eleanor Roosevelt believed in service to the community. What organizations help people in your community? Give an example of something you can do to help them.

121. Parts of Speech—Part II

A. Circle the correct choice in parentheses for each *italized* word.

1. Who killed *President Lincoln?*   (subject (direct object))

2. John Wilkes Booth *shot* him in 1865.   ((past tense) past perfect tense)

3. Booth *was* an actor from the South.   (transitive (linking))

4. He was angry about the Civil War, *and* he hated Lincoln.   ((conjunction) preposition)

5. He found out that Lincoln *might* attend the theater that night.   ((auxiliary) transitive)

6. Lincoln admired a famous *actress* in the play.   ((direct object) object complement)

7. The play was *quite* funny.   ((degree) manner)

8. *Suddenly* a shot rang out.   ((adverb) adjective)

9. Booth escaped, but *he* hurt his leg.   ((third person) first person)

10. Lincoln died the day *after* he was shot.   ((preposition) conjunction)

B. On the line supply the information about the *italicized* word(s).

1. *Who* is this book about?   kind of pronoun   _____ [interrogative] _____

2. *This* book is about Lincoln.   kind of adjective   _____ [demonstrative] _____

3. I *will read* it tonight.   tense of verb   _____ [future] _____

4. *He* was the 16th president of the United States.   person of pronoun   _____ [third] _____

5. It was *not* an easy time to be president.   kind of adverb   _____ [negation] _____

6. A *fierce* Civil War broke out over slavery.   part of speech   _____ [adjective] _____

7. The North *and* the South went to war in 1861.   part of speech   _____ [conjunction] _____

8. The Northern army finally *won.*   tense of verb   _____ [simple past] _____

9. *Alas!* Lincoln did not live to rebuild the country.   part of speech   _____ [interjection] _____

10. He died *from* an assassin's bullet.   part of speech   _____ [preposition] _____

122. Periods

> A **period** is used at the end of a declarative or an imperative sentence. Periods are also used after many common abbreviations.
>
> **Gen. D. D. Eisenhower became president and was inaugurated on Jan. 20, 1953.**
> **Please deliver 2 gal. of white paint to 647 S. Prairie Ave. at 8 a.m. on Sat., May 3.**
>
> Periods are not used in abbreviations for metric measures or after the postal abbreviations for states.
>
> **cm = centimeter**   **MI = Michigan**

Add periods where needed in these sentences.

1. Rev. Conklin asked Prof. Angela B. Kingston to speak at the awards luncheon.

2. The ceremony will take place at 1 pm. on Sun, Sept. 17.

3. Please meet in front of the Miller Bldg. at 590 Bell St. at 11:30 am.

4. Dr. Mendoza will pass out the tickets and table assignments then.

5. Everyone from R. F. Kennedy School should attend.

6. My cousin C. J. gave me a great recipe for fruit smoothies.

7. Wash 1½ c. of your favorite berries and peel 1 small banana.

8. Put the fruit in a blender with ½ c. yogurt and 4 oz. milk.

9. Add 6 ice cubes and blend until smooth.

10. Enjoy your frosty treat.

11. The F. W. Williams Container Co. is located in Beloit, WI.

12. They produce 1-gal. pails for the Primer Paint Corp. and other industries.

13. The president of the company is Mrs. Sylvia Bache.

14. She was recently named Employer of the Year by Gov. Stephens.

15. Mr. Bache and their children are proud of her.

16. To get to the zoo, take the No. 9 bus about ¾ mi. south to the Fullerton Ave. stop.

17. Catch the No. 16 bus and go east about 2 mi. to the W. Sheridan Rd. stop.

18. Cross the street and walk about 50 yd. south.

19. I'll meet you Sat. at 2 pm. near the zoo entrance.

20. Let me know by Fri. if you can come.

Name _____

123. Commas in Series, Dates, and Addresses

Commas are used to separate words or groups of words in a series of three or more and to set off parts of dates, addresses, and geographic names.

Illinois produces corn, soybeans, and wheat.

Springfield, Illinois, was Lincoln's home for many years.

Illinois joined the Union on December 3, 1818, as the 21st state.

The John Hancock Building, once the tallest apartment building in the world, is located at 875 North Michigan Avenue, Chicago, Illinois 60611.

A. Insert commas where needed.

1. Silver, mercury, tin, and nickel are metals.
2. These metals are found in the United States, South Africa, and Canada.
3. Coal, oil, and natural gas are fossil fuels.
4. The United States imports petroleum from Canada, Saudi Arabia, and Mexico.
5. Acid rain from the burning of fossil fuels harms plants, animals, and people.
6. Fossil fuels are obtained by drilling, strip-mining, and tunneling.
7. The United States should explore alternative kinds of energy, such as solar power, wind power, and nuclear power.
8. Geysers, volcanoes, and tides are other natural sources of energy.
9. A fuel called methanol can be obtained from wood, coal, and natural gas.
10. In the meantime, people mine coal, dig oil wells, and tap natural gas.

Sn 50
Tin
119

Ag 47
Silver
107.868

Ni 28
Nickel
58.71

B. Rewrite the sentences, inserting commas where needed.

1. The United States adopted the Constitution on September 17 1787.

[The United States adopted the Constitution on September 17, 1787.]

2. Philadelphia Pennsylvania is where the Constitution was written.

[Philadelphia, Pennsylvania, is where the Constitution was written.]

3. Boonesboro Kentucky reportedly was founded by Daniel Boone on April 1 1775.

[Boonesboro, Kentucky, reportedly was founded by Daniel Boone on April 1, 1775.]

4. The White House is at 1600 Pennsylvania Avenue Washington D.C.

[The White House is at 1600 Pennsylvania Avenue, Washington, D.C.]

5. The *Mayflower* landed at what is now Plymouth Massachusetts on December 21 1620.

[The *Mayflower* landed at what is now Plymouth, Massachusetts, on December 21, 1620.]

124. Commas in Letters and with Appositives

Commas are used after the salutation in both social and friendly letters and after the closing in all letters.

> **Dear Aunt Helen,**   *(after salutation)*
>
>   **Thanks for the video games you gave me for my birthday. I play them every day after I finish my homework.**
>
>   **Love,**   *(after closing)*
>   **Bradley**

Commas are used to set off nonrestrictive appositives.

> **William the Conqueror, the first Norman king of England, gained control of England in 1066.**

A. Insert commas where needed.

> **Dear Aunt Marge and Uncle Ralph,**
>
>   **Thanks for taking Billy and me camping last week. It was really fun to visit Yellowstone Park and see the bears and geysers. I hope you can spend Christmas with us again this year.**
>
>   **Love,**
>   **Paula**

B. Insert commas where needed.

1. Queen Elizabeth II, the present queen of England, ascended the throne on February 6, 1952.

2. The queen's father, George VI, had been king from 1936 to 1952.

3. George VI became king when one of his brothers, Edward VIII, abdicated in order to marry Wallis Simpson, an American woman.

4. George VI and Elizabeth, his wife, courageously stayed in London during the bombings of World War II.

5. Queen Elizabeth II is married to Phillip Mountbatten, the Duke of Edinburgh.

6. Prince Charles, her eldest son, is next in line to the throne.

7. Prince Charles has two sons, Prince William and Prince Henry.

8. Diana, the Princess of Wales, died in a tragic automobile accident in Paris in 1997.

9. The elder son of Charles and Diana, Prince William, is second in line for the throne.

10. Over the years some people have wondered whether the English monarchy might end upon the death of the present sovereign, Queen Elizabeth II.

125. Commas with Quotations

> Commas are used to set off short direct quotations from the rest of the sentence. If the quotation is at the beginning of the sentence, place a comma after the last word of the quotation, unless a question mark or an exclamation point is needed.
>
> **"Mexico is the United States' neighbor to the south," said Professor Louis.**
>
> If the quotation is at the end of the sentence, place a comma after the last word before the quotation.
>
> **Professor Louis said, "Mexico is the United States' neighbor to the south."**
>
> If the quotation is divided, use a comma after the first part and before the latter part.
>
> **"Mexico," Professor Louis said, "is the United States' neighbor to the south."**

Insert commas where needed. Not every sentence needs a comma.

1. "Mexico," said Professor Louis, "has a long and rich history."

2. "The original inhabitants of Mexico were Native Americans of various groups, including the Aztecs and the Toltecs," he said.

3. "These indigenous groups built important civilizations," he continued.

4. A student asked, "What happened to those civilizations?"

5. "They changed dramatically," he answered, "when the Spanish arrived, starting in 1492."

6. He stated, "By 1535 Mexico was completely under Spanish control."

7. "During the colonial period many indigenous achievements were forgotten or lost," he said.

8. "What a terrible thing!" a student exclaimed.

9. The professor told the students, "Mexico declared its independence from Spain in 1810."

10. "However," he continued, "Spain did not recognize Mexico's independence until 1821."

11. "Mexico had several forms of government," he explained, "in the following years, including a republic and an empire."

12. One student asked, "What is Mexico like today?"

13. "Nowadays," said the professor, "Mexico is a developing country with deep cultural traditions."

14. "Mexico is rich in mineral wealth, and it is an important manufacturing center," he said.

15. "Tourism is an important business as well," concluded the professor.

126. Commas in Compound Sentences

> A comma is used to separate the clauses of a compound sentence connected by the coordinating conjunction *and, but, or, nor,* or *yet.*
>
> **The Atlantic Ocean is east of the United States, and the Pacific Ocean is west.**

A. Insert commas where needed. If no comma is needed, write **NC** on the line.

_____ 1. The longest river in the United States is the Missouri, but the Nile River is longer.

_____ 2. The Great Lakes compose the world's largest freshwater system, and the Mississippi River is the longest river that flows southward.

_____ 3. The rivers of Japan are short, but many have waterfalls.

_[NC]_ 4. The most important rivers in northern Europe are the Danube and the Rhine.

_____ 5. The Amazon River is the longest river in South America, and the Paraná is the second-longest.

_____ 6. The Congo River is the longest river in sub-Saharan Africa, but the Nile River in Egypt is longer.

_[NC]_ 7. The Yangtze River is the longest river in China and in all of Asia.

_____ 8. People use rivers to generate electricity, and they also use them as a means of transportation.

_[NC]_ 9. Rivers are a source of water for drinking and for the irrigation of crops.

_____ 10. This summer I will sail the Mississippi River, or I will take a cruise on the Amazon.

B. Complete each sentence with a coordinating conjunction and a comma if required.

1. Root beer was a type of herbal tea __[, and/but]__ later it became a soft drink.

2. In England some people eat eggs __[and]__ drink tea for breakfast.

3. Natural spring water is bottled at a spring __[, and]__ it is prized for its mineral content.

4. The syrup for colas was first created as a cure for headaches __[, but]__ now people drink colas anytime.

5. Carbonated drinks first came only in bottles __[, and/but]__ later they became available in cans.

127. Reviewing Commas

Insert commas where needed.

1. The European Renaissance started in Italy, and it spread to all the other countries of Europe.

2. The Renaissance, a reawakening of learning, started in about 1350.

3. During the Renaissance scholars rediscovered classical Greek and Roman writings, and they studied the ancient texts earnestly.

4. Painting, sculpture, and architecture began to change at this time too.

5. Three centers of activity were Rome, Florence, and Venice.

6. In Florence, a city in central Italy, the members of the ruling family were patrons of the arts.

7. The patrons, members of the Medici family, supported many important artists.

8. One of these artists was Michelangelo, a noted painter and sculptor.

9. Michelangelo created beautiful sculptures for the city of Florence, and he created wonderful paintings in Rome.

10. Michelangelo died on February 18, 1564.

11. One person said, "The world has many kings but only one Michelangelo."

12. Other important Renaissance artists are Leonardo da Vinci, Sandro Botticelli, and Raphael.

13. They painted religious subjects, figures from ancient myths, and portraits of contemporary people.

14. Museums around the world exhibit many Renaissance works, and these are greatly admired today.

15. The Renaissance profoundly influenced art, music, and thought.

16. Bob asked, "Have you read the history of the Renaissance?"

17. "Yes," Pam answered, "the Renaissance was the topic of my last report."

18. "The Renaissance," our teacher said, "is an extremely important period in European history."

19. The *Mona Lisa*, da Vinci's most famous painting, can be seen in the Louvre Museum.

20. You can get information on Italy by writing to the Italian Government Travel Office at 630 Fifth Avenue, New York, NY 10111.

128. Exclamation Points and Question Marks

> An **exclamation point** is used at the end of an exclamatory sentence to express a strong emotion or reaction. An exclamation point is also used after an interjection or exclamatory words to express happiness, disgust, pain, agreement, impatience, surprise, sadness, amazement, or other strong emotion.
>
> **What a great gymnast he is!**
> **Oh, no! He fell off the parallel bars.**
>
> A **question mark** is used at the end of a question.
>
> **Who do you think will win the event?**

A. Add an exclamation point or a question mark where needed.

1. Shh! Did you hear that noise?

2. What a great movie that was!

3. We won the game! Hooray!

4. When will you bake the brownies?

5. Hurry up! Don't you want to be on time?

6. Will you babysit tonight? Great!

7. Who made these delicious cookies?

8. How lucky you were!

9. Where are the baby's toys?

10. Quick! Run inside!

B. Add a period, an exclamation point, or a question mark where needed.

1. What is a peninsula?

2. Spain, Italy, and Greece are located on peninsulas.

3. What is the difference between a peninsula and an island?

4. Which state in the United States is made up of a group of islands?

5. Wow! It's really far away from the mainland.

6. Alaska has a group of islands too.

7. Several places on the coast of South Carolina become islands when the tide is high.

8. When the tide is low, they are connected to the mainland by sandbars.

9. No kidding! Can you drive to those islands?

10. Many of the sandbars are quite compact, and a small car can drive on them.

129. Semicolons

A **semicolon** is used to separate the clauses of a compound sentence when they are not separated by a coordinating conjunction such as *and, but,* or *or.* Semicolons are also used to separate items in a series when the items themselves contain commas.

I have read a lot about South America; it has an interesting history.
I have been to Buenos Aires, Argentina; Santiago, Chile; and Montevideo, Uruguay.

A. Rewrite each sentence. Replace the comma and the coordinating conjunction with a semicolon.

1. Simón Bolívar was born in South America, and he was the son of an aristocrat.

   [Simón Bolívar was born in South America; he was the son of an aristocrat.]

2. In 1810 Bolívar joined a revolt against Spain, but his forces were defeated.

   [In 1810 Bolívar joined a revolt against Spain; his forces were defeated.]

3. Bolívar led another revolt in 1817, and this time he liberated Venezuela.

   [Bolívar led another revolt in 1817; this time he liberated Venezuela.]

4. Bolívar fought other battles, and he helped liberate Colombia, Ecuador, and Peru.

   [Bolívar fought other battles; he helped liberate Colombia, Ecuador, and Peru.]

5. Bolívar is remembered as a great hero, and his birthday is a national holiday in Venezuela and Bolivia.

   [Bolívar is remembered as a great hero; his birthday is a national holiday in Venezuela

   and Bolivia.]

B. Insert commas and semicolons where necessary.

1. They visited Rome, Italy; Paris, France; and London, England.

2. Bolívar won battles on June 24, 1821; May 3, 1822; and August 6, 1825.

3. I thanked Mrs. Cabot, my principal; Ms. Caputo, my teacher; and Mr. Bendix, my coach.

4. The teams in the North Division are located in Green Bay, Wisconsin; Chicago, Illinois; Detroit, Michigan; and Minneapolis, Minnesota.

5. My brothers were born on February 3, 1999; April 16, 2001; and October 30, 2003.

Conjunctions, Interjections, Punctuation, Capitalization

130. Colons

> A **colon** is used after the salutation of a business letter.
>
> **Dear Dr. Bradley:**
>
> A colon is also used before a list of items. A colon must never follow a verb.
>
> **You will need these items: wood glue, a screwdriver, and a vise.**
> **You can make a bookcase, a shoe rack, or a step stool.**

Decide whether each sentence needs a colon. If it does, rewrite the sentence, adding the colon in the correct place.

1. We are learning about the following three types of cephalopods octopuses, squids, and cuttlefish.

   [We are learning about the following three types of cephalopods: octopuses, squids,

   and cuttlefish.]

2. Cephalopods are related to these bivalves that you may have eaten scallops, oysters, and clams.

   [Cephalopods are related to these bivalves that you may have eaten: scallops, oysters, and clams.]

3. Cephalopods are found in oceans all over the world in the tropics, at the poles, along the shore, and in the open sea.

   [Cephalopods are found in oceans all over the world: in the tropics, at the poles, along the shore,

   and in the open sea.]

4. These animals can change their colors, their shapes, and their body textures.

   _____

5. They appeared on earth long ago before mammals, before vertebrates, even before most kinds of plants.

   [They appeared on earth long ago: before mammals, before vertebrates, even before most

   kinds of plants.]

131. Quotation Marks

Quotation marks are placed before and after every complete quotation and every part of a divided quotation. Commas and periods go inside the quotation marks. A question mark or an exclamation point goes inside the quotation marks if it is part of the quotation but outside the quotation marks if it is part of the entire sentence.

> **"I'm sorry," said Jake, "but I'm going to be late."**
> **"Can I help you?" asked Marty.   Who said, "The game is over"?**

Quotation marks are used to set off the titles of songs, short stories, poems, magazine articles, newspaper articles, and episodes of television series. Titles of books, magazines, newspapers, movies, plays, operas, TV series, and works of art are printed in italic type. When these titles are handwritten, they are underlined.

> **I read "How to Save the Planet" in *Time* magazine.** (printed title, italic type)
> **He sang "Now" on the TV series <u>Kids</u>.** (handwritten title, underlined)

Rewrite each sentence, adding quotation marks and underlining where needed.

1. Jack Prelutsky's poem The Crocodile appeared in the book Zoo Doings.

   [Jack Prelutsky's poem "The Crocodile" appeared in the book <u>Zoo Doings</u>.]

2. Is The March of the Penguins a good movie? Gracie asked.

   ["Is <u>The March of the Penguins</u> a good movie?" Gracie asked.]

3. She played the song Octopus's Garden from the album Abbey Road.

   [She played the song "Octopus's Garden" from the album <u>Abbey Road</u>.]

4. I didn't know, Tim remarked, that she likes the Beatles.

   ["I didn't know," Tim remarked, "that she likes the Beatles."]

5. The Golden Book of Fairy Tales includes the story The Frog Prince.

   [<u>The Golden Book of Fairy Tales</u> includes the story "The Frog Prince."]

6. Who read the Chicago Tribune article Walrus Fans Sure to Blubber with Joy?

   [Who read the <u>Chicago Tribune</u> article "Walrus Fans Sure to Blubber with Joy"?]

7. Rick said My little brother's favorite book is Where the Wild Things Are.

   [Rick said, "My little brother's favorite book is <u>Where the Wild Things Are</u>."]

8. Oh! exclaimed Andy. That was my favorite book too.

   ["Oh!" exclaimed Andy. "That was my favorite book too."]

9. Tonight's episode of the TV show Champions of the Wild is called Manatee.

   [Tonight's episode of the TV show <u>Champions of the Wild</u> is called "Manatee."]

10. In the book The Old Man and the Sea, Santiago struggles to catch a giant fish.

    [In the book <u>The Old Man and the Sea</u>, Santiago struggles to catch a giant fish.]

132. Apostrophes

An **apostrophe** is used to show possession; to show the omission of a letter, letters, or numbers; and to show the plural of a small letter.

Brad's report is on Jesse Owens's performance at the '36 Olympic games.
The women's book group and the boys' scout troop both meet today.
Don't forget that Mississippi has two *p*'s, four *i*'s, and four *s*'s.

An apostrophe is not used to form the plural of a number or of an abbreviation that does not have periods. Also, an apostrophe is not used to form the plural of a capital letter unless the plural form can be misread,

10s   1940s   URLs   Rs (but I's)

Insert apostrophes where needed.

1. I enjoy Emily Dickinson's poetry.

2. The painting *The Spirit of '76* is by Archibald M. Willard.

3. He recited Longfellow's poem "Paul Revere's Ride."

4. Edgar Allan Poe's middle name is spelled with two *a*'s.

5. I can't remember C. S. Lewis's first name.

6. The moon's orbit around Earth takes about 30 days.

7. The blizzard of '01 is one of this century's storms that we've read about.

8. He's visiting the Zócolo, Mexico City's main plaza.

9. Susan has difficulty writing *r*'s and *z*'s correctly.

10. The Joneses' house was built in the 1970s.

11. I'll open Granddad's present first.

12. Please don't touch Carlos's toys.

13. He didn't write the boys' last names in alphabetical order.

14. My mom couldn't believe that I got all A's on my report card.

15. They've provided the uniforms for all the girls' soccer teams.

16. Atlanta's Summer Olympic Games were in '96.

17. Jen's and Rhonda's entries won top prizes.

18. The ascenders on your *b*'s and *h*'s shouldn't touch the letters above them.

19. Andrew Wyeth's most famous painting is called *Christina's World*.

20. She hasn't read Laura Ruby's book *Lily's Ghosts*.

133. Hyphens

A **hyphen** is used to divide a word at the end of a line when one or more syllables are carried to the next line. It is also used in some compound words and in the numbers from twenty-one to ninety-nine when these numbers are written out.

> **My brother-in-law put himself through college and graduated when he was only twenty-eight.**

Some compounds are hyphenated only when they act as adjectives.

> **I like ice cream, so I bought an ice-cream cone.**

A. Add hyphens to the compounds that normally use them. Check a dictionary if you need help.

1. self-respect
2. attorney general
3. off-line
4. dirt bike
5. sister-in-law
6. blue jay
7. old-fashioned
8. saber-toothed
9. line drive
10. parking lot

B. Add hyphens where necessary. Check a dictionary if you need help.

1. My cousin's father-in-law took his eight-year-old neighbor to the circus, where they saw an amazing high-wire act.

2. In case of an emergency, pack your car with a first-aid kit, a blanket, a good flash-light, and some bottled water.

3. I saw a ruby-throated hummingbird among the forget-me-nots in grand-mother's garden.

4. A month may contain twenty-eight, twenty-nine, thirty, or thirty-one days.

5. The thyroid, a butterfly-shaped gland located in the throat, controls the body's metabolism and energy level.

6. Niagara Falls consists of three fast-flowing waterfalls that lie on the border be-tween Canada and the United States.

7. The happy-go-lucky boy ate at a fast-food restaurant and then walked aim-lessly around town.

8. A mountain lion is a large, powerfully built wildcat that is found in the moun-tainous regions of northwest North America.

9. Romeo and Juliet, Shakespeare's star-crossed lovers, die because of their mis-understandings.

10. All twenty-two members of Mr. Spivak's eighth-grade class chipped in to get him a retirement gift.

134. Capital Letters

Use **capital letters** in these places:

THE FIRST WORD IN A SENTENCE	Help is on its way.
THE FIRST WORD OF A DIRECT QUOTATION	Patrick Henry said, "Give me liberty or give me death!"
PROPER NOUNS AND ADJECTIVES	I went to France last year. Let's buy some Colombian coffee.
TITLES BEFORE A NAME	Let's ask Reverend Washington.
NORTH, SOUTH, EAST, AND WEST WHEN THEY REFER TO SECTIONS OF THE COUNTRY	The South lost the Civil War.
ALL NAMES REFERRING TO DEITIES	The Arabic word for God is *Allah*.
THE BIBLE OR PARTS OF THE BIBLE, AND OTHER SACRED WORKS	The creation story is in Genesis.
THE PRINCIPAL WORDS IN TITLES	Let's watch *Gone with the Wind*.
THE PRONOUN *I*	Phil and I walked home together.
ABBREVIATIONS WHEN CAPITALS WOULD BE USED IF THE WORDS WERE WRITTEN IN FULL	He is Dr. Ahkook Sawlani, M.D.
THE FIRST WORD OF EVERY LINE OF MOST POETRY	Lift ev'ry voice and sing, Till earth and heaven ring . . .

Use the proofreading symbol (≡) under the letters that should be capitalized.

1. louise remarked, "there is a special message about thanksgiving on the bulletin board."

2. the most important leader of the civil rights movement was dr. martin luther king, jr.

3. petra recited langston hughes's "life is fine," and i recited "harlem."

4. the bible, the koran, and the torah are all important sacred works.

5. fred asked, "have you ever been to the smithsonian institution?"

6. *honey, i shrunk the kids* is a really funny movie.

7. my dentist is dr. ron oakdale, d.d.s.

8. the robbery case was tried before judge amos abraham.

9. the west attracted many settlers in the 1800s.

10. pike's peak is in colorado.

Name _____

135. Reviewing Punctuation and Capitalization

A. Write the correct punctuation mark in each box.
On the line write which punctuation mark or marks you used.

ACROSS

____[apostrophe]____ 3. What☐s the longest river in the world?

____[exclamation point]____ 4. Great☐ The Nile is the right answer.

____[comma]____ 5. The address of the wildlife organization is
70 E. Falmouth Highway☐ East Falmouth, MA 02536.

____[colon]____ 6. There are many endangered species☐ rhinoceroses, pandas,
and tigers.

____[comma]____ 7. Anita asked☐ "Do you know who wrote *The Adventures of
Tom Sawyer?*"

____[apostrophe]____ 8. It☐s one of Mark Twain's best-loved works.

DOWN

____[question mark]____ 1. "Where is Puget Sound☐" asked Nancy.

____[colon]____ 2. We learned about Washington state☐ its natural resources,
its history, and its current econmy.

____[commas]____ 5. We went to the top of the Empire State Building☐ took a
boat to the Statue of Liberty☐ and shopped on Fifth Avenue.

____[comma]____ 6. Rockefeller Center is located in New York☐ New York.

B. Use the names of the punctuation marks
in Part A to complete the crossword puzzle.

Name _____

Rewrite each sentence with correct punctuation and capitalization.

11. the abbreviation j.f.k. in our librarys name stands for john fitzgerald kennedy

   [The abbreviation J.F.K. in our library's name stands for John Fitzgerald Kennedy.]

   _____

12. annually the american library association awards the john newbery medal to
   an outstanding childrens book

   [Annually the American Library Association awards the John Newbery Medal to an

   outstanding children's book.]

13. no I havent read the latest winner

   [No, I haven't read the latest winner.]

14. in canada the canadian library association awards a similar prize to a canadian book

   [In Canada the Canadian Library Association awards a similar prize to a Canadian book.]

   _____

15. do you enjoy reading science fiction fantasy or nonfiction

   [Do you enjoy reading science fiction, fantasy, or nonfiction?]

Try It Yourself

Write four sentences about what you studied in school this week.
Be sure to use punctuation and capitalization correctly.

_____

_____

_____

_____

Check Your Own Work

Choose a selection from your writing portfolio, your journal, a work in progress,
an assignment from another subject, or a letter. Revise it, applying the skills you
have reviewed. This checklist will help you.

✔ Have you followed the rules for commas?

✔ Have you used quotation marks with direct quotations
and around titles of short works?

✔ Have you followed the rules for capitalization?

✔ Do your sentences end with correct punctuation marks?

Name _____

136. Subjects and Predicates

A **diagram** is a picture of a sentence. It shows how the words in a sentence relate to each other. A diagram highlights the most important words and clearly indicates the words that go with them.

Start the diagram by drawing a horizontal line. Find the verb in the sentence and write it on the right half of the horizontal line. Find the subject. Write it to the left of the verb. Separate the subject and the verb by a vertical line that cuts through the horizontal line.

A word that describes the subject or the verb is written on a slanting line under the subject or the verb.

SENTENCE: **The graceful swallows flew swiftly.**

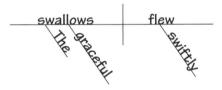

Diagram each sentence.

1. The unhappy baby wailed loudly.

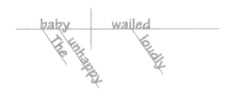

2. The orange cat is sleeping.

3. The hungry children ate quickly.

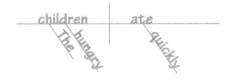

CONTINUED

4. The contest will end tomorrow.

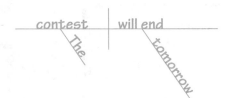

5. The black clouds were approaching rapidly.

6. The lead guitarist sings well.

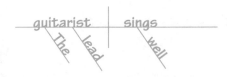

7. The carefree boy whistled happily.

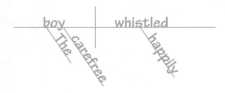

8. The little brown puppy barked excitedly.

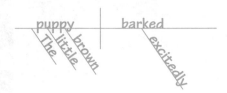

137. Direct Objects and Indirect Objects

In a diagram a direct object is written on the main horizontal line to the right of the verb. It is separated from the verb by a vertical line that touches the horizontal line but does not cut through it.

An indirect object is placed on a horizontal line under the verb and is connected to the verb by a slanting line.

SENTENCE: **The boy gave his mother the large package.**

Diagram each sentence.

1. The principal will award the top students prizes.

2. Kate sent her uncle a thank-you note.

3. This online catalog guarantees its customers prompt delivery.

CONTINUED

4. The cheerful babysitter is teaching the children a new game.

5. Marcus showed me his secret hideout.

6. My cousin lent my big brother his new car.

7. The teacher assigned the noisy students extra homework.

8. Randy's energetic spaniel often chases squirrels.

9. A local citizen wrote the governor a long letter.

Diagramming

138. Subject Complements

In a diagram a subject complement is written to the right of the verb on the main horizontal line. It is separated from the verb by a slanted line that points back toward the subject. The slanted line touches the horizontal line but does not cut through it.

SENTENCE: **Harry Potter is my favorite literary character.**

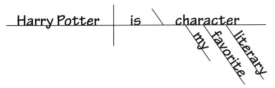

Diagram each sentence.

1. These plates are dirty.

2. The brisk wind felt chilly.

3. Tomorrow will be your lucky day.

4. Abraham Lincoln was very tall.

CONTINUED

Diagramming

5. An okapi is an unusual African mammal.

6. My favorite snack is hot, crunchy popcorn.

7. Those boys look extremely happy.

8. Our class's best speller is she.

9. Mount Rushmore is a popular tourist destination.

10. His choice possession is his new skateboard.

Name _____

139. Appositives

In a diagram an appositive is placed in parentheses to the right of the word it identifies. Words that describe the appositive go under it.

SENTENCE: **The puffin, an arctic sea bird, eats small fish.**

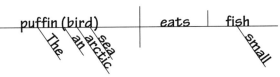

Diagram each sentence.

1. Paul McCartney wrote "Hey Jude," a popular Beatles' song.

2. The American inventor Thomas Edison developed the first phonograph.

3. Mom prepared my favorite dessert, chocolate cake with creamy frosting.

4. Seattle's symbol is the Space Needle, a famous landmark.

5. My little sister enjoys *Sesame Street,* an excellent children's show.

6. Our block party, an annual celebration, will be held tomorrow.

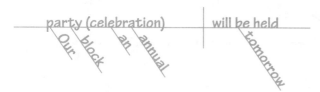

7. Loretta's parents got her a new pet, a golden hamster.

8. My uncle, an award-winning cook, is also a fine mechanic.

9. I bought my friend a birthday present, a new computer game.

10. George Washington, our first president, was once a surveyor.

Diagramming

140. Intensive Pronouns and Reflexive Pronouns

In a diagram an intensive pronoun is placed in parentheses directly to the right of the word it emphasizes. A reflexive pronoun is placed according to its function in the sentence, as the direct object or the indirect object or as the object of a preposition.

SENTENCE: **I will frost the cookies myself.**   SENTENCE: **She wrote herself a note.**

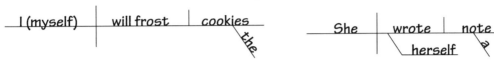

SENTENCE: **The wrestlers weighed themselves regularly.**

Diagram each sentence.

1. The boys made themselves some hot chocolate.

2. Karen herself cleaned the garage.

3. My little brother cannot feed himself yet.

CONTINUED

Diagramming

4. My cousin rebuilt the engine himself.

5. My mother bought herself a new computer.

6. The old cat slowly stretched itself.

7. Karl will cook the whole meal himself.

8. The bird made itself a cozy nest.

9. The coaches themselves will award the prizes.

141. Prepositional Phrases

In a diagram a prepositional phrase goes under the word it describes. The preposition goes on a slanting line. The object of the preposition goes on a horizontal line connected to the line with the preposition. Any words that describe the object go under it.

SENTENCE: **The man at the podium is speaking about the new gym.**

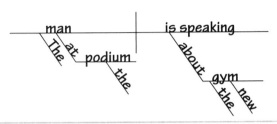

Diagram each sentence.

1. The flowers in the blue vase need water.

2. The cat is sunning itself on the back porch.

3. Martha hid the presents under her bed.

4. I made myself a big pot of tomato soup.

Diagramming

5. The boy with the blue bike is my next-door neighbor.

6. A woman on the bus was carrying a bunch of red balloons.

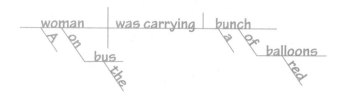

7. The ball crashed through the garage window.

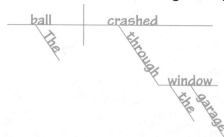

8. The members of the cleanup committee got coupons for free pizzas.

9. Mrs. Silva, the president of the parents' club, made a special announcement.

142. Compound Sentence Parts

In a diagram compound sentence parts are placed on separate horizontal lines, with the coordinating conjunction on a dashed line between them. The horizontal lines are placed in their correct position in the diagram.

SENTENCE: **Mom and I picked tomatoes and corn and served them for dinner.**

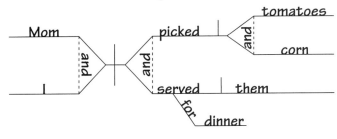

SENTENCE: **My favorite dish is roast chicken and stuffing with onions and sausage.**

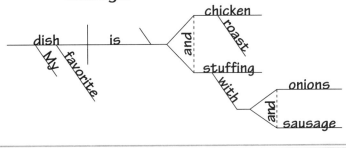

Diagram each sentence.

1. Cockatoos and macaws are kinds of parrots.

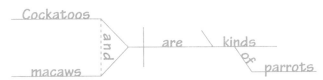

2. Tim and Trudy went to the zoo and the aquarium.

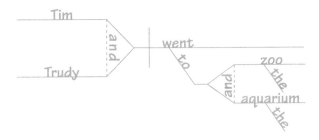

3. Benjamin Franklin was a diplomat and an inventor.

Diagramming

4. My dad and I washed the car and cleaned the garage.

5. The teacher gave Rob and Helen instructions and encouragement.

6. He went to the library and borrowed a book about pandas.

7. My aunt and my uncle bought a boat and sailed to Aruba and Barbados.

8. My grandfather worked hard and became a successful engineer.

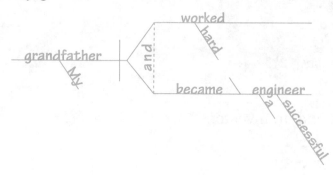

143. Compound Sentences

In a diagram each independent clause of a compound sentence is diagrammed separately on its own horizontal line. The coordinating conjunction is placed between the clauses on a dashed vertical line that connects the left edges of horizontal lines.

SENTENCE: **The sky was very cloudy, but we started the game anyway.**

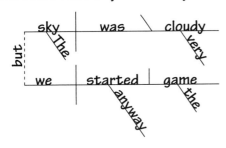

Diagram each sentence.

1. I could not find the information in the library, but I located it online.

2. The party will be held in the gym, and everyone should wear a costume.

3. We can see that movie in the theater, or we can rent the DVD.

4. Ray did his homework before dinner, but Rita watched TV.

5. An ostrich is a large creature, but it has a small brain.

6. I received the application yesterday, and I completed it immediately.

7. Mia bought Luke a birthday present, and she gave it to him today.

8. You should bring the cushions inside, or the rain will ruin them.

144. Interjections

In a diagram an interjection is placed on a line that is separate from the rest of the sentence. The line is above, to the left, and parallel to the main horizontal line.

SENTENCE: **Help! The rope is breaking!**

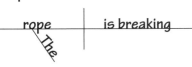

Diagram each sentence.

1. Ah! That breeze feels wonderful.

2. Oh! You startled me.

3. Well! I will never do that again.

4. Sh! We should not spoil the surprise.

CONTINUED

Diagramming

5. Hey! You splashed water on me.

6. Good, we finally finished our chores!

7. Oops! My ice cream fell in the sand.

8. Yikes! You are going to be late for practice.

9. Wow! Your new skateboard is great!

10. Gee, that is an enormous fish!

Diagramming

145. Adverb Clauses

In a diagram an adverb clause goes on its own horizontal line under the independent clause. The conjunction is placed on a slanted line that connects the two clauses. The line goes from the verb in the adverb clause to the word in the independent clause that the adverb clause describes, which is usually the verb.

SENTENCE: **After we planted the garden, we had cookies and lemonade.**

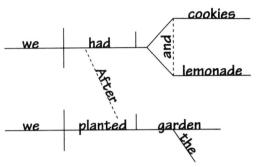

Diagram each sentence.

1. They will not finish the job until they buy more paint.

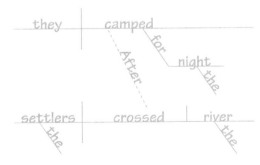

2. After the settlers crossed the river, they camped for the night.

3. Although the house was attractive, the Smiths did not buy it.

CONTINUED

Diagramming

4. John made himself a sandwich before he left for the game.

5. We were late because we had a flat tire.

6. Laura made the toast while Anna scrambled the eggs.

7. When Wes dropped the ball, Jerry scored the final run.

8. The children played tag in the yard until they were called for dinner.

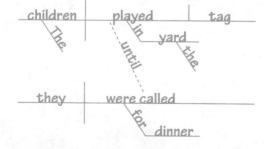

Diagramming

146. Diagramming Review

> In a diagram each part of a sentence has its own place.

Diagram each sentence.

1. The boys went into the kitchen and made themselves some lunch.

2. The famous architect Frank Gehry designed the new museum

3. She cannot finish the puzzle unless she finds the lost piece.

4. My brother and I built the birdhouse ourselves, but Dad hung it in the tree.

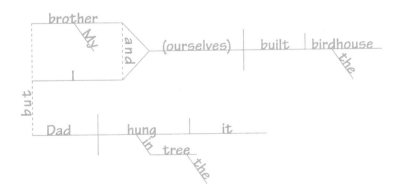

CONTINUED

Diagramming

Name _____

5. Yikes! The cat is on the roof, and it will not come down.

6. The whole school was proud when the chess team won the tournament.

7. My aunt is an attorney and the author of three law books.

8. Will Frank send Harry an e-mail or will he call him on the phone?

9. Grizzly bears are large and powerful, and they can be very aggressive.

10. William Howard Taft, our 27th president, became Chief Justice of the Supreme Court.

Diagramming

ADJECTIVES

An **adjective** points out or describes a noun.

An **article** points out a noun. *A, an* and *the* are articles. *The* is the **definite article.** *A* and *an* are **indefinite articles:** *The* boy ate *an* apple and *a* pear.

A **demonstrative adjective** points out a specific person, place, or thing. *This, that, these,* and *those* are demonstrative adjectives: *this* book, *those* pencils.

A **descriptive adjective** tells about age, size, shape, color, origin, or another quality of a noun. A descriptive adjective usually comes before the noun it describes. It may also follow a linking verb: It was a *sunny* morning. The popcorn tasted *great*.

An **indefinite adjective** refers to any or all members of a group. Indefinite adjectives include *all, another, any, both, each, either, few, many, more, most, much, neither, other, several,* and *some: both* boys, *either* girl.

An **interrogative adjective** is used in questions. *What, which,* and *whose* are interrogative adjectives: *Whose* book is this?

A **possessive adjective** shows possession or ownership. The possessive adjectives are *my, your* (singular), *his, her, its, our, your* (plural), and *their: my* car, *your* motorcycle: *her* hat, *your* book.

Some adjectives tell exactly how many: *ten, twenty-five, third, twelfth.* Some adjectives tell about how many: *many, few, several, some.*

See also **antecedents, comparisons, prepositions, sentences, subject-verb agreement.**

ADVERBS

An **adverb** modifies a verb, an adjective, or another adverb.

- An **adverb of affirmation** tells that something is positive or gives consent or approval: The music is *certainly* beautiful.

- An **adverb of degree** answers the question how much or how little: The boy is *quite* tall.

- An **adverb of manner** answers the question how, or in what manner: Jason draws *well.*

- An **adverb of negation** expresses a negative condition or refusal: The door is *not* locked.

- An **adverb of place** answers the question where: Sit *here* by the gate.

- An **adverb of time** answers the question when or how often: It rained *yesterday.*

A negative idea is expressed by using one negative word. This negative word may be *no, not, none, never,* or *nothing.* These words should be used only in sentences that have no other negative words: I do not have *any* (not *no*) apples.

See also **clauses, comparisons, prepositions.**

ANTECEDENTS

The noun to which a pronoun or possessive adjective refers is its **antecedent.** A pronoun or a possessive adjective must agree with its antecedent in person and number. A third person singular pronoun or possessive adjective must agree in gender also.

See also **adjectives, pronouns.**

CAPITALIZATION

Capital letters are used for many purposes, including the following:

- The first word of a sentence—The bell rang.

- Proper nouns and proper adjectives—Betsy Ross, American flag

- An abbreviation if the word it stands for begins with a capital letter—Rev. for Reverend

- The first word and the name of a person addressed in the salutation of a letter and the first word in the complementary close of a letter—Dear Marie, Yours truly,

- The principal words in the titles of books, plays, works of art, and poems—*A Tale of Two Cities, Romeo and Juliet, Mona Lisa,* "Fire and Ice"

- The first word of a direct quotation—Mother said, "It's time for my favorite television program."

- Titles when used before a person's name—Thank you, Professor Higgins.

- North, East, South, West when they refer to sections of the country or the world. They are not capitalized when they refer to directions—the old West. He drove west on Main Street.

- The pronoun *I*

- Names referring to deities or sacred works—God, the Bible

- Two-letter state postal abbreviations—MA, NY, CA

- The first word of each line of most poetry

CLAUSES

A **clause** is a group of related words that contains a subject and predicate.

A **dependent clause** does not express a complete thought and cannot stand alone. A dependent clause, together with an independent clause, forms a complex sentence.

- An **adverb clause** is a dependent clause used as an adverb. Adverb clauses are usually introduced by conjunctions such as *although, as, after, because, before, for, since, that, though, unless, until, where,* and *while: After we had canoed down the river,* we went to a clambake on the beach.

An **independent clause** expresses a complete thought. An independent clause can stand alone as a sentence: After we had canoed down the river, *we went to a clambake on the beach.*

See also **sentences.**

COMPARISONS

Many adjectives and adverbs can be used to compare two or more persons, places, things, or actions.

- The **positive degree** describes one or more persons, places, things, or actions: The *tall* boy ran *fast.*

- The **comparative degree** compares two persons, places, things, or actions. Form comparatives by adding *-er* to the positive degree or by putting *more* or *less* before the positive degree: The *younger* child cried *more sadly.*

- The **superlative degree** compares three or more persons, places, things, or actions. Form superlatives by adding *-est* to the positive degree or by putting *most* or *least* before the positive degree: The *tallest* boy ran *most quickly.*

Few, fewer, and *fewest* are used to compare count nouns. *Little, less,* and *least* are used to compare noncount nouns: *little* money, *few* dimes.

CONJUNCTIONS

A conjunction is used to connect words, phrases, or clauses in a sentence.

A **coordinating conjunction** connects similar words, phrases, or clauses. *And, or, but, nor,* and *yet* are coordinating conjunctions: Todd *and* Cindy will come early to help us. They will research on the Internet *and* in the library. We left on time, *but* we got there late.

See also **clauses, sentences.**

CONTRACTIONS

A **contraction** is two words written as one with one or more letters omitted. An apostrophe is used to show the omission of a letter or letters: *we're, she's, don't, I'll.*

INTERJECTIONS

An **interjection** expresses a strong or sudden emotion, such as delight, disgust, pain, agreement, impatience, surprise, sorrow, or wonder: *Oh! Shh! Ouch! Wow!*

MOOD

Mood shows the manner in which an action or state of being is expressed.

- The **indicative mood** of a verb is used to make a statement or ask a question. Most sentences are in the indicative mood: Where *are* you *going?* Tom *is going* to the park.

- The **emphatic form** of the indicative mood gives special force to a simple present or past tense verb. To make an emphatic form, use *do, does,* or *did* before the base form of the verb: I *do want* to go! She *does have* a pony. They *did find* the treasure.

- The **imperative mood** is used to express a command or a request. To form the imperative, use the base form of the verb. The subject of an imperative sentence is understood to be the pronoun *you:* Please open the door. A command can be given in the third person by using *let's* before the base form of a verb: *Let's* measure the rug.

- The **subjunctive mood** is used in several ways: to express a wish or a desire; to express a request, a command, or a suggestion after the word *that;* or to express something that is contrary to fact (not true). For the verb *be,* the common forms of the subjunctive are *be* and *were:* I wish my dog *were* better behaved. My dad suggested that I *be* patient with her. If I *were* more patient, I would train her.

NOUNS

A **noun** is the name of a person, place, or thing.

An **abstract noun** names a quality, a condition, or a state of mind. An abstract noun names something that cannot be seen or touched: *anger, idea, spirit.*

A **common noun** names any one member of a group of persons, places, or things: *queen, city, church.*

A **concrete noun** names a thing that can be seen or touched: *brother, river, tree.*

A **count noun** names something that can be counted: *nickels, bags, emotions.*

A **noncount noun** names something that cannot be counted: *money, luggage, fear.*

A **plural noun** names more than one person, place, or thing: *boys, berries, geese.*

A **possessive noun** expresses possession or ownership.

- To form the possessive of a singular noun, add *-'s* to the singular form: *architect's.*

- To form the possessive of a plural noun that ends in *s*, add an apostrophe to the plural form: *farmers'.*

- To form the possessive of a plural noun that does not end in *s,* add *-'s* to the plural form: *children's.*

- To show separate possession, add *'-s* to each noun: *Meg's* and *Mike's* dogs.

- To show plural possession, add *-'s* to the last noun only: *Jack* and *Jill's* pail.

A **proper noun** names a particular person, place, or thing. A proper noun is capitalized: *Queen Elizabeth, London, Westminster Abbey.*

A **singular noun** names one person, place, or thing: *boy, river, berry.*

PREPOSITIONS

A **preposition** is a word that shows the relationship between a noun or a pronoun and some other word in a sentence. The **object of a preposition** is the noun or pronoun that follows the preposition: The huge mountain lion leaped *through* (preposition) the tall *grass* (object of the preposition).

A **prepositional phrase** is a phrase that is introduced by a preposition.

- An **adjective phrase** is used as an adjective and modifies a noun: The cabin *in the woods* burned down.

- An **adverb phrase** is used as an adverb and generally modifies a verb: The river flows *into the sea*.

PRONOUNS

A **pronoun** is a word that takes the place of a noun or nouns.

A **demonstrative pronoun** points out a definite person, place, or thing. *This, that, these,* and *those* are demonstrative pronouns: *This* is mine. *Those* are yours.

An **indefinite pronoun** refers to any or all of a group of persons, places, or things. Among the indefinite pronouns are *all, another, both, each, either, few, many, neither, nothing, several, some,* and pronouns beginning with *any* or *every: Each* wants to be on the team. *Both* must pass physicals. *Anybody* can join.

An **intensive pronoun** (*myself, yourself, himself, herself, itself, ourselves, yourselves, themselves*) is used to emphasize a preceding noun or pronoun: I *myself* cooked the entire dinner.

An **interrogative pronoun** is used to ask a question. The interrogative pronouns are *who, whom, which, what,* and *whose:* To *whom* does this belong?

An **object pronoun** is used as the direct or indirect object of a verb or as the object of a preposition. The object pronouns are *me, you, him, her, it, us,* and *them:* Mary called *her* yesterday. Joe gave *them* directions. The call was for *him.*

Personal pronouns have different forms.

- A personal pronoun shows **person:** the speaker (**first person**), the person spoken to (**second person**), or the person spoken about (**third person**). The first person pronouns are *I, me, mine, we, us,* and *ours.* The second person pronouns are *you, yours.* The third person pronouns are *he, him, his, she, her, hers, it, its, they, them,* and *theirs.*

- A personal pronoun shows **number:** it is **singular** when it refers to one person, place, or thing. The singular pronouns are *I, me, mine, you, yours, he, him, his, she, her, hers, it,* and *its.* A personal pronoun is **plural** when it refers to more than one person, place, or thing. The plural pronouns are *you, yours, they, them,* and *theirs.*

- The third person singular pronoun shows **gender:** it can be **masculine** (*he, him, his*), **feminine** (*she, her, hers*), or **neuter** (*it, its*).

A **possessive pronoun** shows possession or ownership. The possessive pronouns are *mine, yours, his, hers, its, ours,* and *theirs.* A possessive pronoun takes the place of a noun and its possessive adjective. Although possessive pronouns show ownership, they do not contain apostrophes: The new skates are *hers.*

A **reflexive pronoun** (*myself, yourself, himself, herself, itself, ourselves, yourselves, themselves*) can be used as a direct or an indirect object or as the object of a preposition: She made *herself* a sandwich. The kitten saw *itself* in the mirror.

A **subject pronoun** is used as a subject or a subject complement. The subject pronouns are *I, you, he, she, it, we,* and *they: We* played soccer. The goalie was *he.*

See also **antecedents, comparisons, sentences, subject-verb agreement.**

PUNCTUATION

An **apostrophe** (') is used as follows:

- To show ownership: the *cook's* hat, the *girls'* horses

- To replace letters or numbers that are omitted: *wasn't, '76*

- With *s* to show the plural of small letters: Mind your *p's* and *q's.*

- With *s* to show the plural of a capital letter that could be misread: *I's*

A **colon** (:) is used as follows:

- After the salutation in a business letter: Dear Sir:

- Before a list when terms such *as follows* or *the following* are used: We bought the following: *eggs, limes, bread, sugar.*

Commas (,) are used to make written material clearer. Among the comma's uses are the following:

- To separate words or groups of words in a series of three or more: We saw elephants, giraffes, hyenas, and monkeys.

- To set off parts of dates, addresses, or geographical names: January 1, 2003; 321 Spring Road, Atlanta, Georgia

- To set off words in direct address: Josie, I'm so pleased that you called me this morning.

- After the word *yes* or *no* when it introduces a sentence: Yes, I agree with you completely.

- To set off direct quotations, unless a question mark or an explanation point is required: "We have only vanilla and chocolate today," he said in an apologetic tone.

- Before a coordinating conjunction in a compound sentence: She called his name, but he didn't answer her.

- After the salutation of a friendly letter and the closing of all letters: Dear Ben, Sincerely,

- To separate a nonrestrictive appositive from the rest of the sentence: Chicago, the biggest city in Illinois, is not the state capital.

An **exclamation point** (!) is used after an exclamatory sentence and after an interjection: Wow! What a celebration that was!

A **hyphen** (-) is used as follows:

- To divide a word at the end of a line whenever one or more syllables are carried to the next line

- In the words for numbers from twenty-one to ninety-nine and to separate the parts of some compound words: *soldier-statesman, half-baked* plan

A **period** (.) is used at the end of a declarative or an imperative sentence and after initials and some abbreviations: Pres. J. F. Kennedy was from Massachusetts.

A **question mark** (?) is used at the end of a question: What time is it?

Quotation marks (". . .") are used as follows:

- Before and after every direct quotation and every part of a divided quotation: "Let's go shopping," said Michiko. "I can go with you," Father said, "after I have eaten lunch."

- To enclose titles of short stories, poems, and magazine articles. Titles of books, magazines, newspapers, movies, TV shows, and works of art are usually printed in *italics* or are underlined: I read "The Lost City" in *Newsweek.*

A **semicolon** (;) is used as follows:

- To separate the clauses of a compound sentence when they are not separated by a conjunction: I can't ride my bike; the wheel is damaged.

- To separate phrases or clauses that contain commas: We went to Paris, France; Rome, Italy; and London, England.

SENTENCES

A sentence is a group of words that expresses a complete thought. A sentence must contain a subject and a predicate.

- An **appositive** is a noun that follows another noun in a sentence and renames it: Kanisha Taylor, the *president* of our class, will make the first speech.

- A **direct object** is the receiver of the action of a verb. A noun or an object pronoun can be used as a direct object: Nat helped *him* with his homework.

- An **indirect object** is a noun or pronoun that tells to whom, to what, for whom, or for what the action in a sentence is done. A sentence must have a direct object in order to have an indirect object: I gave *him* a present.

- The **predicate** tells something about the subject. The **simple predicate** is a verb or verb phrase: Teresa *waved* to the child from the window. The **complete predicate** is the verb with all its modifiers, objects, and complements: Teresa *waved to the child from the window*. A **compound predicate** is two or more simple predicates: Teresa *waved* and *shouted*.

- The **subject** names the person, place, or thing a sentence is about. The **simple subject** is a noun or pronoun: The *man* is riding his bike. The **complete subject** is the simple subject with all its modifiers: *The tall young man* is riding his bike. A **compound subject** is two or more simple subjects: The *man* and the *woman* are riding bikes.

- A **subject complement** is a word that completes the meaning of a linking verb in a sentence. A subject complement may be a noun, an adjective, or a pronoun: Broccoli is a green *vegetable*. The sea will be *cold*. The best player is *he*.

A **complex sentence** contains one independent clause and one or more dependent clauses: *The party had started before we arrived.*

- A **dependent clause** does not express a complete thought and cannot stand alone: *before we arrived.*

- An **independent clause** expresses a complete thought: *The party had started.*

A **compound sentence** contains two or more independent clauses.

- The clauses in a compound sentence are usually connected by a coordinating conjunction preceded by a comma: Sometimes Jane drives to work, *but* today she took the train.

- A semicolon may be used to separate the clauses in a compound sentence: She left on time; the train was late.

A **declarative sentence** makes a statement. A declarative sentence is followed by a period: The sun is shining.

An **exclamatory sentence** expresses strong or sudden emotion. An exclamatory sentence is followed by an exclamation point: What a loud noise that was!

An **imperative sentence** gives a command or makes a request. An imperative sentence is followed by a period: Go to the store. Please pick up the papers.

An **interrogative sentence** asks a question. An interrogative sentence is followed by a question mark: Where is my pen?

A **simple sentence** contains one subject and one predicate. Either or both may be compound. Any objects and/or complements may also be compound: *Ivan* and *John* argued with the grocer. The baby *walks* and *talks* well. Wear your *hat, scarf,* and *gloves.*

Sentence order is the sequence of the subject and verb in a sentence.

- When the verb in a sentence follows the subject, the sentence is in **natural order:** The *settlers planted* the seeds.

- When the main verb or a helping verb in a sentence comes before the subject, the sentence is in **inverted order:** Across the plain *marched* the tired *soldiers.*

See also **clauses, subject-verb agreement.**

SUBJECT-VERB AGREEMENT

A subject and a verb must always agree.

- In the present tense a verb that agrees with a singular noun ends in *-s:* A duck *swims.*

- Indefinite pronouns such as *anyone, anything, everybody, no one, nobody, nothing, one, somebody,* and *something* and indefinite adjectives such as *another, each, either, neither,* and *other* are always singular and require a verb that agrees with a third person singular subject: *Everyone* in this class *works* hard. *Each* girl *is trying* her best.

- Indefinite pronouns and indefinite adjectives such as *all, few, many, several,* and *some* are generally plural: *Few look* carefully before turning. *Both* puppies *are eating* their treats.

- When a sentence begins with *there* and a form of the verb *be,* the subject follows the verb. The verb must agree with the subject: There *is* a *fly* on the wall. There *are bees* in the hive.

- Compound subjects connected by *and* usually require a verb that agrees with a plural subject: My brother *and* sister *are waiting.*

- Some nouns have the same form in the singular and the plural. The sense of the sentence determines whether the subject is singular or plural: Many *deer* live in these woods. A young *deer* is eating the plants in our garden.

TENSES

The tense of a verb shows the time of its action.

- The **simple present tense** tells about an action that happens again and again: I *play* the piano every afternoon.

- The **simple past tense** tells about an action that happened in the past: I *played* the piano yesterday afternoon.

- The **future tense** tells about an action that will happen in the future; the future is formed with the present and the auxiliary verb *will* or the verb phrase *going to* with a form of the verb *be*: The piano recital *will be* on Sunday. I *am going to play* two songs.

- The **present progressive tense** tells what is happening now; the present progressive tense is formed with the present participle and a form of the verb *be:* He *is eating* his lunch now.

- The **past progressive tense** tells what was happening in the past; the past progressive tense is formed with the present participle and a past form of the verb *be:* He *was eating* his lunch when I saw him.

- The **future progressive tense** tells what will be happening in the future. The future progressive tense is formed with the present participle and *will be, is going to be,* or *are going to be:* The teacher *will be grading* the tests this evening.

- The **present perfect tense** tells about a past action that is relevant to the present: I *have lived* here for six years now.

- The **past perfect tense** tells about a past action that happened before another past action: I *had lived* in Memphis for a year before I moved here.

VERBS

A **verb** is a word that expresses action or state of being.

An **intransitive verb** has no receiver of the action. It does not have a direct object: The sun *shone* on the lake.

A **linking verb** links a subject with a subject complement (a noun, a pronoun, or an adjective).

- The verb *be* in its many forms *(is, are, was, will be, have been, etc.)* is the most common linking verb: He *is* happy. They *are* students. The winner *was* she.

- The verbs *appear, become, continue, feel, grow, look, remain, seem, smell, sound,* and *taste* are also considered linking verbs: This *tastes* good. She *became* president.

Modal auxiliary verbs such as *may, might, can, could, must, should,* and *would* are used to express permission, possibility, ability, necessity, and obligation: You *should* hurry. We *might be* late.

A verb has four **principal parts:** the present, the present participle, the past, and the past participle.

- The present participle is formed by adding *-ing* to the present: *walking, running.*

- The simple past and the past participle of regular verbs are formed by adding *-d* or *-ed* to the present: *raked, raked; walked, walked.*

- The simple past and the past participle of irregular verbs are not formed by adding *-d* or *-ed* to the present: *ran, run.*

A **transitive verb** expresses an action that passes from a doer to a receiver. The receiver is the direct object of the verb: The dog *ate* the *bone.*

A **verb phrase** is a group of words that does the work of a single verb. A verb phrase contains one or more auxiliary or helping verbs *(is, are, has, have, will, can, could, would, should, etc.)* and a main verb: She *had forgotten* her hat.

VOICE

In the **active voice** the subject of a sentence is the doer of the action: Betty *wrote* a poem.

In the **passive voice** the subject of a sentence is the receiver of the action: The poem *was written* by Betty.